A VHDL
Synthesis Primer

J. BHASKER

AT&T Bell Laboratories, Allentown, PA

Star Galaxy Publishing
1058 Treeline Drive, Allentown, PA 18103

Published by:

Star Galaxy Publishing
1058 Treeline Drive, Allentown, PA 18103
Phone: 610-391-7296

Cover design: *Gail Hallenbeck*

Printed in the United States of America

10 9 8 7 6 5 4 3 2

Library of Congress Catalog Card Number: 95-73048

ISBN 0-9650391-0-2

"Where there is a will, there is a way"

"If at first you fail, try, try, try again"

- My Mom

This book is dedicated to her for all the hard work she has done in raising five children.

Contents

Chapter 4

Model Optimizations, 97

Chapter 5

Verification, 115

Chapter 6
Modeling Hardware Elements for Synthesis, 135

Preface

Here is a practical and useful guide to VHDL synthesis. To many, synthesis appears like a black-box; a design described in VHDL goes in, and out comes a gate-level netlist. Designers are not comfortable with this black-box approach. To take full advantage and usefulness of a synthesis system, it is important to understand the transformations that occur during the synthesis process. The purpose of this book is to expose the black-box myth by describing the transformations that occur during the synthesis process from a hardware description language model to a netlist; VHDL is used as the modeling language.

VHDL is one of the dominant hardware description languages that is used for synthesis. VHDL was originally developed for the Department of Defense, but subsequently it also became an IEEE and an ANSI standard. Its flexibility lies in the fact that it is a very broad language containing constructs that can be used to describe sequential behavior, concurrent behavior, and structure, including data abstraction, all using one modeling language. The language provides support for modeling the system hierarchically and also supports top-down and bottom-up design methodologies. A digital system and its subsystems can be described at any level of abstraction ranging from the architecture level to the gate level. Precise simulation semantics are associated with all the language constructs and therefore models written in this language can be verified using a VHDL simulator.

Synthesis, in general, has a different meaning to different people. In this book, I refer to synthesis of a design described in VHDL; this design describes combinational logic and or sequential logic. In case of sequential logic, the clocked behavior of the design is expressly described. This precludes talking about logic synthesis (a design described in terms of primitive gates) and about high-level synthesis (behavior specified with no clocking information). The synthesis process transforms this VHDL model into a gate-level netlist. The target netlist is assumed to be a technology-independent representation of the modeled logic. The target technology contains technology-independent generic blocks such as logic gates and register-transfer level (RTL) blocks, such as arithmetic-logic-units and comparators. The succeeding phases of a synthesis process, which are technology translation (that is, mapping of generic gates to specific parts in a library) and module binding (that is, building RTL blocks using primitive gates) are not described in this book.

It is difficult to write a book on synthesis due to its rapidly evolving nature. In this book, I have therefore tried to provide the basic information that will hold true by and large. I have tried to stay clear of ambiguous topics including implementation-specific issues. Because of the richness of the VHDL language, there may be more than one way to describe a certain behavior. This book suggests one or two such modeling styles that are synthesizable. Again, not all constructs in the language can be synthesized since VHDL was designed to be a simulation language. Therefore, in this book, I have tried to show constructs that would be supported by a majority of synthesis systems.

I have also tried to avoid mentioning the various features of vendor-specific synthesis tools. However, there are certain cases when it becomes necessary to show an example of an implementation. In such a case, I have showed how the feature is implemented in the ArchSyn (version 14.0) synthesis system developed at AT&T Bell Laboratories.

CAUTION: Not all available synthesis systems may support the VHDL constructs described in this book. The ArchSyn-specific features described in this book are for illustrative purposes only. For more details on specific features of the ArchSyn system, or on any other synthesis system, the reader is urged to consult the respective vendors' documentation.

This book assumes that the reader knows the basics about the VHDL language. The book is targeted to electrical engineers, specifically circuit and system designers, who are interested in understanding the art of synthesis. The book does not try to explain any of the synthesis algorithms. My belief is that by understanding what results to expect from synthesis, a designer will be able to control the quality of the synthesized designs by writing optimized behavioral models. This is because the synthesized structure is very sensitive to the way in which a certain model is written.

The VHDL used in this book is based on IEEE Std 1076-1993. The IEEE standard package for model interoperability, STD_LOGIC_1164 (IEEE Std 1164) is also used in many examples in this book.

Book organization

Chapter 1 gives a brief overview of the VHDL language. It is not intended to be a tutorial or a complete description of the language. The reader is urged to read any other text book on VHDL for further details or refer to the VHDL Language Reference Manual (LRM), the official bible for VHDL.

The basics of the synthesis process are described in Chapter 2. The basics include topics such as what is a wire, a flip-flop or a state, how are the sizes of objects determined, and so on.

Chapter 3 describes the mapping of VHDL constructs to logic gates. It gives examples of how combinational logic is inferred and how these get transformed into basic gates and interconnections. Styles for modeling synchronous designs are also described along with examples for modeling asynchronous preset and clear, synchronous preset and clear, multiple clocks, and multiple-phase clocks.

Occasionally it becomes necessary to use predesigned blocks in a design. Chapter 3 further describes how to model structure, including the capability to model partial structure in a behavior model.

Chapter 4 describes powerful techniques that can be applied to a VHDL model to provide quality synthesized netlists. The optimizations described in this chapter may be performed automatically by a synthesis system; if not, it may have to be performed manually by the designer to achieve quality results.

Having synthesized a VHDL model, it is often necessary to validate the synthesized netlist with the input model. Chapter 5 provides test-bench writing strategies that can be used to verify the synthesis results. Because VHDL is not specifically designed to be used as a synthesis language, differences do arise between pre- and post-synthesis simulation results. This chapter explains the cause of many such discrepancies.

Chapter 6 describes how VHDL constructs are collectively used to model hardware elements. While Chapter 3 describes the mapping of VHDL to logic gates, this chapter describes the opposite scenario, which is, how to model a hardware element for synthesis using VHDL. Elaborate examples are provided for many common hardware elements, such as multiplexers, counters, decoders and arithmetic-logic-units.

In order to illustrate a subset of VHDL supported for synthesis by a typical synthesis system, Appendix A gives a construct by construct description of what is supported by the ArchSyn synthesis system. However, such a subset may vary between different synthesis systems.

Appendix B gives a listing of an arithmetic package, STD_LOGIC_ARITH, that is based on the IEEE standard package STD_LOGIC_1164. This package is used in many of the examples described throughout the book.

Appendix C describes the logic gates in a generic library that are used in the synthesized circuits described in this book.

The synthesized netlists shown in this book are NOT optimized netlists; thus the logic shown in some cases may be suboptimal. This is acceptable since the purpose of this book is to show the transformation of VHDL to gates and not that of demonstrating logic optimization techniques. Some of the netlists have been optimized purposely so that the netlist could be captured as a figure in the book.

In all the VHDL descriptions that appear in this book, reserved words are in **boldface**. Occasionally ellipsis (. . .) is used in VHDL source to indicate code that is not relevant to that discussion. All examples that are described in this book have been synthesized using the ArchSyn synthesis system and validated using a native VHDL simulator.

Certain words in the text have been written using Courier font, such as if statement and wait statement; this was done so as not to confuse these with their normal English meaning. This convention is applied only for words that cause confusion with the English language. Words such as "variable" in variable assignment and "report" in report statement are not set in a separate font.

Acknowledgments

I would like to thank and acknowledge the following individuals for providing invaluable comments and constructive suggestions that has resulted in a much improved book:

- Doug Smith, Kevin Duke, Brett Graves from Intergraph Electronics.
- Jim Vellenga from Viewlogic Systems.
- Rob Anderson from VLSI Technology.
- J. Vijay Kumar from Hong Kong University of Science and Technology.
- Mourad Takla, Daniel Johnson, Kanchan Mhatre, Carlos Roman, John Jansen, Sriram Tyagarajan from AT&T Bell Laboratories.
- Rich Hatcher from Texas Instruments.

I am very grateful to these individuals for their help.

I would also like to acknowledge Hao Nham, Jean Dussault and Mike Tong for their constant encouragement and in providing a flexible and conducive atmosphere at AT&T Bell Laboratories for making this book possible.

My wife, Geetha, and my two rajahs, Arvind and Vinay, deserve a very special thanks for their continued support, understanding and encouragement throughout the development of this book. The motivation and driving force for this book also comes from my family, especially from my two rajahs who are very proud to have a Dad whose book is sold at a local bookstore.

J. Bhasker

January, 1996

Chapter 1

Language Basics

This chapter provides a very brief introduction to the VHDL language. It is intended to act as a refresher on VHDL and is not intended to be a comprehensive description of the language and does not describe all its features. The reader is urged to read a text on VHDL or the VHDL Language Reference Manual for further details. Details of a synthesizable subset of VHDL is given in Appendix A.

1.1   About VHDL

VHDL is a hardware description language intended for documenting and modeling digital systems ranging from a small chip to a large system. It can be used to model a digital system at any level of abstraction ranging from the architectural level down to the gate level.

The language was initially developed specifically for Department of Defense VHSIC (Very High Speed Integrated Circuits) contractors. However, due to an overwhelming need in the industry for a standard hardware description language, the VHSIC Hardware Description Language (VHDL) was selected and later approved to become an IEEE standard called the IEEE Std 1076-1987. The language was updated again in 1993 to include a number of clarifications in addition to a number of new features like report statement and pulse rejection limit. The examples in this book are based on this version of the language called the IEEE Std 1076-1993.

1.2   Design units

There are five kinds of design units provided in VHDL.

a. *Entity declaration*: An entity declaration describes the interface of the design to its external environment, that is, it describes the ports (inputs, outputs, etc.) through which the design communicates with other designs.

```
library SYNTH;
    -- Library clause declares the design library SYNTH.
use SYNTH.STD_LOGIC_ARITH.all; -- Use clause imports all declarations in
    -- package STD_LOGIC_ARITH into the design unit that follows it.
entity FILTER4 is
    port (XIN, XD1, XD2, XD3: in UNSIGNED (3 downto 0);
          YOUT: out UNSIGNED (3 downto 0));
    -- Declarations may also be present here.
end FILTER4;
    -- The entity FILTER4 has four input ports and one output port.
```

b. *Architecture body*: An architecture body describes the composition or functionality of a design. This could be described as a mix of sequential behavior (behavioral style), concurrent behavior (dataflow style), and components (structural style). A design may have more than one architecture body, each describing a different composition, that is, using a different style of design. An architecture body is always associated with an entity declaration that provides its interface.

```
architecture A1 of FILTER4 is
    -- This is the declarative part:
    constant K0: UNSIGNED (3 downto 0) := "0111";
    constant K1: UNSIGNED (3 downto 0) := "0101";
```

```
            constant K2: UNSIGNED (3 downto 0) := "0011";
            constant K3: UNSIGNED (3 downto 0) := "0100";
        begin
            -- This part contains concurrent statements:
            YOUT <= (K0 * XIN + K1 * XD1) + (K2 * XD2 + K3 * XD3);
            -- The "* " and the "+ " operators are defined in
            -- package STD_LOGIC_ARITH.
        end A1;
        -- Architecture name is A1, and its interface is defined by the
        -- entity declaration FILTER4.
```

c. *Configuration declaration*: A configuration declaration is used to specify the bindings of components present in an architecture body to other design entities. An entire hierarchy of a design, that is, the bindings that link all the design entities in a hierarchy, can also be specified using the configuration declaration.

```
        configuration COMB of FILTER4 is
            for A1
            end for;
        end COMB;
        -- Configuration COMB selects architecture A1 with entity FILTER4.
```

d. *Package declaration*: A package declaration is a repository to store commonly used declarations.

```
        library SYNTH;
        use SYNTH.STD_LOGIC_ARITH.all;
        package OVERLOAD is
            function "and" (L, R: UNSIGNED) return UNSIGNED;
        end OVERLOAD;
        -- Package OVERLOAD contains one function declaration.
```

e. *Package body*: A package body is always associated with a package declaration and contains subprogram bodies, along with other declarations.

```
        package body OVERLOAD is
            function "and" (L, R: UNSIGNED) return UNSIGNED is
                alias LOT: UNSIGNED (1 to L'LENGTH) is L;
                alias ROT: UNSIGNED (1 to R'LENGTH) is R;
                variable RES: UNSIGNED (1 to L'LENGTH);
            begin
                assert L'LENGTH = R'LENGTH;

                for J in LOT'RANGE loop
                    RES(J) := LOT(J) and ROT(J);
```

```
    end loop;

    return RES;
  end "and";
end OVERLOAD;
-- Package body for package OVERLOAD contains the function's body.
```

The minimum design units required to model a design is an entity declaration and one architecture body.

1.3   Data objects

A data object holds a value or a sequence of values of a certain type. There are four classes of data objects.

a.   *Constant*: A constant holds a value of a specified type. It is set once in a constant declaration, and its value cannot be changed later.

```
constant LINELENGTH: NATURAL := 132;
-- Constant LINELENGTH is of the predefined integer subtype NATURAL
-- and its value is 132.
```

b.   *Variable*: A variable also holds a value of a specified type. It can be assigned a value using a variable assignment statement.

```
-- Example of a variable declaration:
variable RES: UNSIGNED (1 to L'LENGTH) := (others => '0');
-- Variable RES is of type UNSIGNED with size L'LENGTH and has a
-- default value of all zeros.
```

c.   *Signal*: A signal has a current value and a set of future projected values. A future value can be assigned to a signal using a signal assignment statement.

```
-- Example of a signal declaration:
signal SBOX, ABOX: INTEGER := 5;
-- Two signals ABOX and SBOX are of type INTEGER and their
-- initial value is 5.
```

d.   *File*: A file contains a sequence of values of a specified type. Values can be written to or read from using procedures.

-- Example of a file declaration:
file STROBE: TEXT **open** WRITE_MODE **is** "./strobe.dat";
-- File STROBE is to be opened in write-only mode and is associated
-- with the physical file "./strobe.dat".

1.4 Data types

A data type represents a collection of values. The following data types are available in VHDL.

a. *Enumeration type*: Values of this type are defined by the user.

   type FDS **is** (ADD, SUB, GT, EQ);
   -- The enumeration type FDS contains four user-defined values.

b. *Integer type*: Values of this type are integer numbers.

   type SBOX_TYPE **is range** 0 **to** 31;
   -- SBOX_TYPE is an integer type with values in the range 0 through 31.

c. *Physical type*: Values of this type represent measurement of some physical quantity.

   type TV_TIME **is** 0 **to** 20_000
      units
         hours;
         days = 24 hours;
      end units TV_TIME;
   -- TV_TIME is a physical type that can have units of hours and days.

d. *Floating point type*: Values of this type are real numbers.

   type SWING **is range** −30.0 **to** +30.0;
   -- Type SWING is a floating point type with real numbers
   -- in the range −30.0 through +30.0

e. *Array type*: An object of this type represents a collection of elements of the same element type.

   type UNSIGNED **is array** (NATURAL **range** <>) **of** BIT;
   -- UNSIGNED is an unconstrained array type, each element is of type BIT.

f. *Record type*: An object of this type represents a collection of elements, possibly of different types.

```
type CHECKING is
  record
     DATE: STRING (1 to 6);
     DOLLARS: NATURAL;
  end record CHECKING;
-- CHECKING is a record type with two elements, DATE
-- and DOLLARS.
```

g. *Access type*: Values of this type represent pointers to other objects.

```
type FDS_PR is access FDS;
-- FDS_PTR is an access type that contain addresses that point to objects
-- of type FDS.
```

h. *File type*: Contains a sequence of values of a specific type.

```
file BIT_PAT is file of BIT;
-- BIT_PAT is a file type that contains a sequence of values of type BIT.
```

Subtypes

A *subtype* is a type with a constraint.

```
subtype BOX_ARR is UNSIGNED (0 to 15);
-- BOX_ARR is a subtype of the type UNSIGNED with an index
-- constraint of 0 to 15.
```

1.5   Design description

A design is described using one or more concurrent statements in an architecture body. A concurrent statement executes based on events in its input list, and thus the order of concurrent statements within an architecture body is not important. The following concurrent statements are available.

a. *Block statement*: A block statement is used to represent a partition of a design.

BLAB: **block** (HANDLE)
begin
    TOG <= **guarded** BOG **after** 5 ns;
end block BLAB;
-- Block statement has a label BLAB. A guard expression,
-- HANDLE, is present. Whenever HANDLE is true, BOG is
-- assigned to signal TOG after 5 ns. If HANDLE is false, signal
-- TOG retains its previous value.

b. *Concurrent procedure call statement*: The specified procedure is called whenever an event occurs on an input signal parameter.

ADDER (FIRST => GUMP, SECOND => HUMP, RESULT => LUMP);
-- Procedure ADDER is called when there is an event on signal GUMP or
-- HUMP, assuming that FIRST and SECOND are input signal parameters.

c. *Concurrent assertion statement*: The assertion is checked whenever an event occurs on a signal used in the assert expression.

assert (CLK = '0' **and** PCK = '1') **or** (CLK = '1' **and** PCK = '0')
    report "CLK and PCK are overlapping."
    severity ERROR;
-- Assertion is checked on every event that occurs on signals CLK and PCK.

d. *Concurrent signal assignment statement*: The signal assignment statement executes whenever there is an event on a signal that is used in the right-hand-side expression. The value of the right-hand-side expression is then assigned to the left-hand-side signal or aggregate after the specified delay. If no delay is specified, a delta delay is assumed. A delta delay is an infinitesimally small delay that is used for ordering events that occur at the same time.

RX_LINK_CODE(0 **to** 5) <= "011001" **after** 3 ns;

e. *Component instantiation statement*: A component instantiation represents a child component of a design. The component is evaluated whenever an event occurs on any of the signals connected to its input ports.

L0: NOR2 **port map** (A => S1, B => S2, Z => SET);
-- L0 is the component label, NOR2 is the component. Assuming
-- component ports A and B are input ports, this component is
-- executed whenever an event occurs on signals S1 or S2.

f.   *Generate statement*: This statement is executed at elaboration time. The execution either causes replication of concurrent statements or causes conditional selection of concurrent statements.

```
GEN_BANK: if NEED_FF generate
   process
   begin
      wait until CLK = '1';
      Q <= DATA_IN;
   end process;
end generate GEN_BANK;
-- GEN_BANK is the label for the generate statement. If NEED_FF is true, the
-- process statement is included in the description. If value is false, the process
-- statement is not included in the description.
```

g.   *Process statement*: A process statement is used to describe the behavior of a design using sequential statements. These statements execute sequentially. The following sequential statements are available.

1.   *Wait statement*: The wait statement causes the process, or the calling process, to suspend.

```
wait for 15 ns;
```

2.   *Report statement*: The report statement prints a message and reports a severity level to the simulator.

```
report "This branch of code is executed"
   severity WARNING;
```

3.   *Assertion statement*: If assertion is false, a message is printed and a severity level is reported to the simulator.

```
assert TOG > 15
   report "TOG is less than or equal to 15"
   severity NOTE;          -- NOTE is the severity level.
```

4.   *Signal assignment statement*: The value of the expression on the right-hand-side is assigned to the left-hand-side signal or an aggregate after the specified delay (if no `after` clause is present, delta delay is assumed. A delta delay is an infinitesimally small delay).

```
PAR <= A xor (B xor C) after 2.1 ns;
```

5.   *Variable assignment statement*: The value of the expression on the right-hand-side is computed and immediately assigned to the left-hand-side variable or an aggregate.

```
                    RESULT := A(K) or A(J);
```

6. *Procedure call statement*: The specified procedure is called.

    ```
    PROPAGATE_DELAY (IN_SIG => Q, OUT_SIG => PROP_Q,
                     DELAY => DLY);
    ```

7. *If statement*: If condition is true, the corresponding set of sequential statements are executed.

    ```
    if DOLLARS < 20 then
        report "Fees will be charged"
            severity ERROR;
    end if;
    ```

8. *Case statement*: Depending on the value of the branch expression, the corresponding set of sequential statements are executed.

    ```
    case FDS_VAR is
        when ADD =>
            Z <= A + B;
        when SUB =>
            Z <= A – B;
        when GT =>
            Z <= A > B;
        when EQ =>
            Z <= A = B;
    end case;
    ```

9. *Loop statement*: The execution of the loop statement causes the statements within the loop to be iterated the specified number of times. A loop statement can be a for-loop, a while-loop or a repeat-forever-loop.

    ```
    -- This is an example of a for-loop:
    for K in 1 to L loop
        SUM := SUM + K;
    end loop;
    ```

10. *Next statement*: Causes the next iteration of the specified loop to be executed. This statement can only be present within a loop statement.

    ```
    next LAB1 when SUM > 10;
    -- Executes the next iteration of loop LAB1 if specified condition is true.
    ```

11. *Exit statement*: Causes the specified loop to be exited. This statement can only be present within a loop statement.

> **exit when** SUM = TOG − 2;
> -- Exits innermost loop if specified condition is true.

12. *Return statement*: Causes the subprogram that contains this return statement to terminate.

> **return** TO_BITVECTOR(46, 6);
> -- Returns the value of the expression to the calling process or subprogram.

13. *Null statement*: Does not perform any action.

> **null**;

1.6 Design libraries

A *design library* is a place in the host environment (*host environment* is the system that provides for VHDL compilation and simulation) where compiled descriptions of design units are stored. A *design file* may contain one or more design units. After successful compilation, compiled design units are stored in a design library that is designated as a working library. Each design library is assigned a logical name (a logical name is a name by which the design library will be referenced in VHDL models) and one of the libraries must be designated as the working library. The design library designated as the working library also has the logical name WORK.

In addition, a predefined design library STD is always present in a host environment. The design library STD contains the predefined packages STANDARD and TEXTIO. The host environment may also provide a design library IEEE that stores IEEE standardized packages, for example, STD_LOGIC_1164.

1.7 Simulating a model

Once all design units related to a complete design have been compiled, the top-level design entity or its configuration is selected for simulation. A simulator then proceeds through the following three stages:

a. Elaboration: Expands the hierarchy down to a set of behavioral models.

b. Initialization: Signals are initialized and processes are executed until they all wait.

c. Event-based simulation: Simulation starts from time 0 and simulation progresses based on events, until no more events are present, or TIME'HIGH is reached (TIME'HIGH is the maximum value for type TIME as defined in the predefined package STANDARD).

1.8   Synthesizing a model

This is the topic for the rest of this book.

❑

Chapter 2

Synthesis Basics

VHDL is a hardware description language that can not only describe hardware at the gate level and the register-transfer level (RTL), but also at the behavioral level using abstract data types. This makes translating a design described in VHDL to logic gates a non-trivial process.

This chapter explains the basics involved in the mapping of the VHDL model to logic gates. It shows what VHDL objects become the value carriers in hardware. VHDL types play an important role in determining the bit-width of a particular object; the mechanics of how bit-widths are computed is explained in this chapter. This chapter also shows that a mapping mechanism is necessary to map the literals in VHDL to values necessary to represent hardware.

2.1   *What is synthesis?*

Synthesis is the process of constructing a gate-level netlist from a model of a circuit described in VHDL.[1] Figure 2-1 shows such a process. A synthesis program may alternately generate a RTL netlist, which is comprised of register-transfer level blocks such as flip-flops, arithmetic-logic-units, and multiplexers, interconnected by wires. In such a case; a second program called the RTL module builder is necessary. The purpose of this builder is to build, or acquire from a library of predefined components, each of the required RTL blocks in the user-specified target technology.

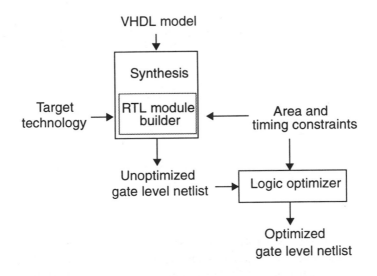

Figure 2-1 The synthesis process.

Having produced a gate-level netlist, a logic optimizer reads in this netlist and optimizes the circuit for the user-specified area and timing constraints. These area and timing constraints may also be used by the module builder for appropriate selection or generation of RTL blocks.

In this book, we assume that the target netlist is at the gate level. The logic gates used in the synthesized netlists are described in Appendix C. The module building and logic optimization phases are not described in this book.

---

1. This is the definition used in this book.

Figure 2-2 shows the basic elements of VHDL and the elements used in hardware. A mapping mechanism or a construction mechanism has to be provided that translates the VHDL elements into their corresponding hardware elements. Questions to ask are:

- How does a data type translate to hardware?
- How are literals mapped to logic values?
- How do data objects map to hardware?
- How are statements translated to hardware?

The following sections discuss these mappings in more detail.

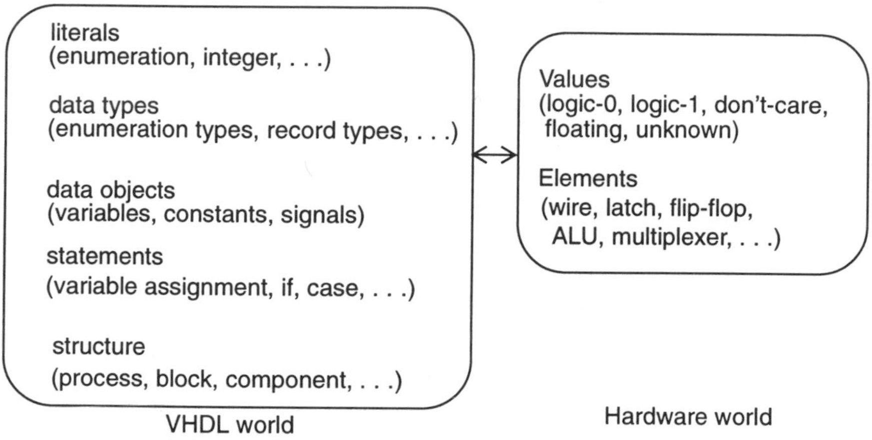

VHDL world

literals
(enumeration, integer, . . .)

data types
(enumeration types, record types, . . .)

data objects
(variables, constants, signals)

statements
(variable assignment, if, case, . . .)

structure
(process, block, component, . . .)

Hardware world

Values
(logic-0, logic-1, don't-care,
 floating, unknown)

Elements
(wire, latch, flip-flop,
 ALU, multiplexer, . . .)

Figure 2-2 The two worlds of synthesis.

2.2 Synthesis in a design process

VHDL is a hardware description language that allows a designer to model a circuit at different levels of abstraction, ranging from the gate level, RTL level, behavioral level to the algorithmic level. Thus a circuit can be described in many different ways, not all of which may be synthesizable. Confounding this is the fact that VHDL was designed primarily as a simulation language and not as a language for synthesis. Consequently, there are many constructs in VHDL that have no hardware counterpart, for example, an assertion statement. Also there is no standardized subset of VHDL for synthesis.

Because of these problems, different synthesis systems support different VHDL subsets for synthesis. Since there is no direct object in VHDL that means a latch or a flip-flop, each synthesis system may provide different mechanisms to model a flip-flop or a latch. Each synthesis system therefore defines its own subset of VHDL language including its own personalized modeling style.

Figure 2-3 shows a circuit that is described in many different ways using VHDL. A synthesis system that supports synthesis of styles A and B may not support that of style C. This implies that typically synthesis models are non-portable across different synthesis systems. Style D may not be synthesizable at all.

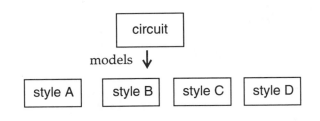

Figure 2-3 Same behavior, different styles.

This limitation creates a severe handicap because now the designer not only has to understand the VHDL language, but also has to understand the synthesis-specific modeling style before a model can be written. The ideal design process shown in Figure 2-4 can no longer be followed for VHDL synthesis.

The problem with this design process is that if the behavioral model is written without knowing the synthesis modeling style, only during the synthesis phase will the designer learn about the synthesis-specific modeling restriction and style for synthesis. A model rewrite may be necessary at this point. Also a lot of time may have been wasted in the "Write model" -> "Compile VHDL" -> "Simulate" -> "Edit model" loop. Instead, the design process shown in Figure 2-5 has to be followed for VHDL synthesis. A synthesis methodology checker is needed to check if the model being written is compatible for synthesis or not, and also this must be done within the first simulation loop. In this way, after the simulation results have been verified, a verified synthesizable model exists, which can then be synthesized.

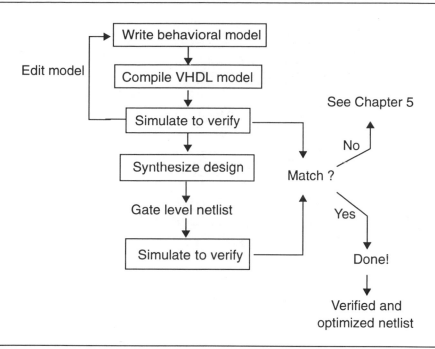

Figure 2-4 Typical design process.

2.3   *Value holders for hardware modeling*

VHDL provides two classes of data objects, signal and variable, that can be used to model the basic value holders in hardware. The basic value holders in hardware are:

- wire
- flip-flop (an edge-triggered flip-flop)
- latch (a level-sensitive flip-flop)

In VHDL, a signal, or a variable declared in a process, retains its value through the entire simulation run, thus inferring memory. However, this is too general for synthesis. Here is an example of a variable that is used as a temporary and therefore need not be a candidate for a memory element.

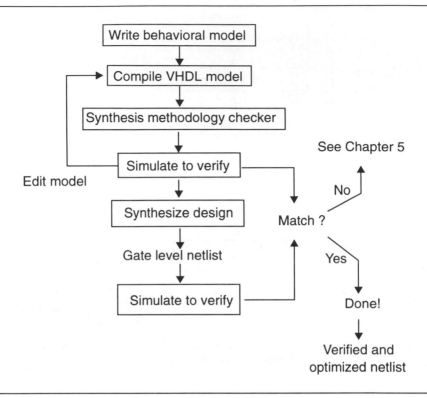

Figure 2-5 New design process.

```
signal CAR, BAR, FAR, SAR: BIT;
. . .
NO_MEMORY: process (BAR, CAR, FAR)
   variable TAR: BIT;
begin
   TAR := BAR and CAR;
   SAR <= TAR or FAR;
end process;
```

Variable TAR is assigned in the first statement and then used in the right-hand-side expression of the second statement. VHDL semantics indicate that variable TAR retains its value through the entire simulation run. However, it is not necessary to store the value of TAR as a memory element in hardware, since it is assigned and used immediately. Figure 2-6 shows the logic generated.

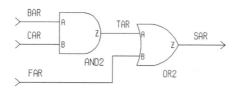

Figure 2-6 Variable TAR is a wire.

Let us look at another example. In this case, the signal TAR is used before its assignment.

```
signal CAR, BAR, FAR, TAR, SAR: BIT;
. . .
IS_IT_A_LATCH: process (BAR, CAR, FAR)
begin
    SAR <= TAR or FAR;
    TAR <= BAR and CAR;
end process;
```

The semantics of this process is very clear in VHDL. Whenever an event occurs on signal BAR, CAR, or FAR, execute the process. Since signal TAR is used before its assignment, signal TAR has to hold its value during repeated executions of the process, thus inferring memory. However, it is not clear how to build a latch for TAR because the signal TAR is not assigned a value under the control of any condition. The ArchSyn synthesis system will not create a latch in this case but will generate the circuit shown in Figure 2-7. Signal TAR is synthesized to a wire again. However, for simulation results to match between pre- and post- synthesis, the signal TAR must be also be in the sensitivity list of the process. More of this is discussed in Chapter 5.

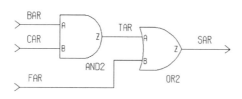

Figure 2-7 No latch for signal TAR.

Here is an example where a latch is inferred.

```
signal SAT, SOUT, ANT: BIT;
...
LATCH: process (SAT, ANT)
   variable FOX: BIT;
begin
   if SAT = '0' then
      FOX := ANT;
   end if;

   SOUT <= not FOX;
end process;
```

The variable FOX is not assigned in the else-branch of the `if` statement. Consequently, a latch is inferred for FOX since it needs to retain its value when the condition SAT='0' is false. The circuit synthesized in shown in Figure 2-8.

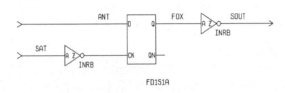

Figure 2-8 Variable FOX is a latch.

How is a flip-flop inferred? It depends on the modeling style being followed and the context under which a variable or a signal is assigned. This and other examples for flip-flop and latch inferencing are discussed in the next chapter. A memory can be modeled as an array of flip-flops or latches.

2.4   *Logic value system*

The common values used in modeling hardware are:

- logic-0
- logic-1
- high-impedance
- don't-care

- unknown

These values are not defined explicitly in VHDL. The literal '0' in VHDL may or may not infer a logic-0 value. The literal 'Z' may or may not infer a high-impedance (or tristate) value. Associating an interpretation for literals in VHDL is left to the designer. Also different mappings may exist from a literal to a hardware value. For synthesis purposes, this mapping needs to be explicitly provided in a form that a synthesis system can understand. The mapping of VHDL literals to the synthesis logic values is provided in the ArchSyn synthesis system by using a special attribute, called ENUM_TYPE_ENCODING.

2.5 Computing bit-widths

In VHDL, an object declaration specifies the type of the object. The size of an object, that is, the corresponding number of bits in hardware, is determined from its type. Given a signal declaration,

> **signal** DAK: INTEGER **range** 10 **to** 31;

what should the size of DAK be, that is, how many bits does signal DAK represent in hardware? The following sections describe how this is determined.

2.5.1 Integer types

The number of bits required for an integer type object is the minimum number of bits needed to hold the largest integer value. The bit representation for an integer can represent either an unsigned number or a signed number. If the integer type object can take a negative integer value, then the object is said to contain signed numbers. A signed number is represented using two's complement form. If the object has only non-negative values, then the object is said to hold unsigned numbers. Here are some examples.

> **signal** AX: INTEGER **range** 0 **to** 15;

> **type** MYINT **is range** −128 **to** +15;
> **variable** BOX: MYINT;

> **subtype** M1 **is** POSITIVE **range** 25 **downto** 5;
> **variable** CAT: M1;

Signal AX is an unsigned integer of 4 bits. AX contains unsigned numbers because it can hold only non-negative values. It is of size 4 bits since this is the minimum number of bits needed to encode the largest integer value, which is 15. BOX is a signed integer of 8 bits. Eight bits are needed, at the minimum, to represent the largest integer value, which is − 128 in two's complement form. Variable CAT is an unsigned number of size 5 bits.

In hardware, signal AX is a vector with range 3 down to 0, variable BOX is a vector with range 7 down to 0, and variable CAT is a vector with range 4 down to 0. The convention of using a descending range with the rightmost index of 0 is specific to the ArchSyn synthesis system. The leftmost bit is the most significant bit. For example, AX(3) and CAT(4) are the most significant bits for signal AX and variable CAT respectively.

In the above examples, the size of objects could be easily determined. What about the following variable?

> **variable** ARB: INTEGER;

What should the size (number of bits) for ARB be? The VHDL language specifies that type INTEGER must at least represent 32 bits. This is an overdesign for synthesis. The ArchSyn system, in such a case, automatically determines the maximum size of variable ARB by performing a dataflow analysis of the model. For example, given the signal assignment statement,

> ARB <= BAR + RUB;

if BAR and RUB are of size 5 bits, ARB will be computed to be of size 6 bits.

2.5.2   Type BIT_VECTOR

The predefined type BIT_VECTOR defines an array of bit values, where a bit is either a '0' or a '1'. The ArchSyn synthesis system interprets the bit value '0' as representing logic-0 and bit value '1' as logic-1 in hardware. Each bit in a bit-vector is represented as one bit in hardware. The size of an object of this type is, thus, directly determined from the size of the array. Here are some examples.

> **signal** RED: BIT_VECTOR (7 **downto** 0);
> **variable** DHA: BIT_VECTOR (0 **to** 3);

```
subtype REST is BIT_VECTOR (26 downto 15);
variable LAP: REST;
constant CONE: BIT_VECTOR := "001";
```

Signal RED is an object of size 8, whose index ranges from 7 down to 0. Variable DHA is of size 4, with its index ranging from 0 to 3. Variable LAP is of size 12, with its index ranging from 26 through 15. The size of constant CONE is determined from the size of the constant value, which is 3, and its index ranges from 0 to 2.

VHDL does not provide any information on which bit of a bit-vector is to be treated as the most significant bit. But such information is necessary for performing arithmetic operations. In the ArchSyn system, values of type BIT_VECTOR represent unsigned numbers and the leftmost bit is treated as the most significant bit. In the previous examples, RED(7), DHA(0), LAP(26) and CONE(0) are the most significant bits.

A value of type BIT_VECTOR can also be made to represent a signed number. This can be accomplished by using a package in which the operands of an arithmetic or a relational operator are treated as signed numbers. For example, here is a declaration for the "+" operator overloaded function.

```
function "+" (L, R: BIT_VECTOR) return BIT_VECTOR;
```

By writing the function body in which the operands are treated as signed numbers, an object of type BIT_VECTOR can then be interpreted as a signed number within the function.

2.5.3   Enumeration types

An enumeration type specifies a user-defined set of values. These values can either be symbolic values, that is, identifiers, or character literals. Here is an example.

```
type SUMMER is (MAY, JUNE, JULY, AUG, SEPT);
signal DAC: SUMMER;
. . .
DAC <= JULY;
```

What is the size of signal DAC? The most common way to compute the size of an enumeration type is to compute the number of bits needed to encode the maximum position number of a literal in the enumeration type. Remember that in VHDL, every enumeration literal has a position number associated with it. The first enumeration literal in an enumeration type has position number 0, the next literal to its right has the position number 1, and so on. So in the case of signal DAC, the number of bits needed is 3. This is because the largest position number in the enumeration type SUMMER is that of the literal SEPT, which is 4. The value of an enumeration literal is decided by its corresponding position number. This implies that the enumeration literal MAY is a 3-bit value "000", JUNE represents the value "001", and so on. In the above example, DAC is being assigned the value "010".

Using the above-specified encoding technique, the predefined type BOOLEAN has a size of one bit, with the literal FALSE representing logic-0, and the literal TRUE representing logic-1.

This encoding of an enumeration type is consistent with the simulation semantics for this type. However, quite often, it may be desirable to specify a different encoding for the enumeration literals. The two common cases where this may be useful are in:

- state encoding of a finite state machine
- encoding of an unknown, a don't-care, or a high-impedance value.

State encoding

Here is a VHDL code fragment.

```
type FSM_STATE is
                (RESET, APPLY, WAITS, CLEAR, SEND, COMPLETE);
signal CURR_ST, NEXT_ST: FSM_STATE;
. . .
case CURR_ST is
  when RESET =>
    NEXT_ST <= CLEAR;
. . .
```

This code describes part of the behavior of a finite state machine. Using the encoding scheme specified earlier, signals CURR_ST and NEXT_ST would be of size 3 bits and the enumeration literals would be encoded as RESET with "000", APPLY with "001", WAITS with "010", and so on.

However in finite state machine synthesis, it is well known [Reference 16. in "Bibliography"] that different encoding schemes produce different hardware representations of a finite state machine behavior. In such a case, the designer may be interested in specifying a different encoding for the enumeration literals.

In VHDL, there is no explicit mechanism for specifying such an encoding. In the ArchSyn system, such an encoding is specified using an attribute of the enumeration type. Here is an example.

> **attribute** ENUM_TYPE_ENCODING: STRING;
> **attribute** ENUM_TYPE_ENCODING **of** FSM_STATE: **type**
>   **is** "000001 000010 000100 001000 010000 100000";

An attribute called ENUM_TYPE_ENCODING is first declared using an attribute declaration. Then using an attribute specification, a string containing the encoded values for each enumeration literal is specified in their respective order; the first encoded value "000001" corresponds to the first enumeration literal RESET, the second encoded value "000010" corresponds to the second enumeration literal APPLY, and so on. In this encoding mechanism, the size of the type is determined by the number of bits specified in the encoding for each of its literals. In this example, the number of bits for the type FSM_STATE is thus 6 bits. The ArchSyn system uses this encoding to synthesize the finite state machine, thereby producing a possibly more efficient implementation.

Using the above encoding in the signal assignment statement in the finite state machine example, the ArchSyn system infers that the value "001000" is assigned to signal NEXT_ST. Also NEXT_ST is of size 6 bits. If the explicit encoding is not present, signal NEXT_ST is then of size 3 bits, and is assigned a value of "011".

The explicit encoding mechanism has to be used with caution since it may create differences in pre- and post- synthesis simulation results. This is because the mechanism used to specify the encoding is not a standard mechanism that a VHDL simulator understands. The encoding is specified purely for synthesis purposes only. See Chapter 5 concerning differences that may arise due to this user-defined encoding.

2.5.4 Encoding metalogical values

In modeling hardware, it is customary to define representations for the unknown, don't-care and high-impedance values. An unknown value (quite often, the value 'U') is usually used to specify unknown input values, which is useful during initial setup of a circuit. A don't-care value (quite often the value 'X' or 'D') is used to specify a don't-care value, that is, a value that can either be a '0' or a '1'. A high-impedance value (often the value 'Z') is used to set a signal to a high-impedance value, for example, in a bus so that another signal may also drive the bus.

However, such representations are not predefined in the VHDL language, and are open to different interpretations. The unknown, don't-care and high-impedance values are called *metalogical values*. In VHDL, there are no explicit reserved words or declarations that can be used to specify the metalogical values.

For a synthesis system, it is desirable to provide a mechanism that explicitly specifies the mapping of VHDL literals to correspond to the metalogical values. In the ArchSyn synthesis system, such a mapping is provided using the ENUM_TYPE_ENCODING attribute. There are five values that a VHDL literal can be mapped to in hardware:

- 0: logic-0
- 1: logic-1
- U: unknown
- D: don't-care
- Z: high-impedance

Here is an example of an enumeration type declaration.

type MIDAS_VALUES **is** (MIDAS_U, MIDAS_0, MIDAS_1, MIDAS_Z);

A designer may interpret the literal MIDAS_U to represent an unknown value, MIDAS_0 as logic-0, MIDAS_1 as logic-1, and MIDAS_Z as a high-impedance value. For synthesis, this information needs to be communicated through the VHDL model. In the ArchSyn system, the ENUM_TYPE_ENCODING attribute is used to pass this information. For example, the following attribute specification can be used with the type MIDAS_VALUES.

attribute ENUM_TYPE_ENCODING **of** MIDAS_VALUES: **type**
is "U 0 1 Z";

The ArchSyn system reads this special attribute specification and interprets that the enumeration literal MIDAS_U corresponds to a U value (unknown) for synthesis, the enumeration literal MIDAS_0 corresponds to a 0 value (logic-0) for synthesis, and so on. More important is the fact that a variable or a signal of the type MIDAS_VALUES needs to be represented using only 1 bit in hardware. Here is an example.

```
variable ROY: MIDAS_VALUES;
. . .
ROY := MIDAS_0;        -- Assignment-1.

if RESET = '0' then
   ROY := MIDAS_Z;    -- Assignment-2.
end if;
```

The ArchSyn system interprets the variable ROY to be of size 1 bit. Assignment-1 is interpreted as an assignment of logic-0 value to variable ROY (since the literal MIDAS_0 is encoded as a 0). Assignment-2 is interpreted as an assignment of a high-impedance value to ROY (since the literal MIDAS_Z is encoded as a Z).

If the ENUM_TYPE_ENCODING attribute specification is not present, variable ROY is then of size 2 bits, since 2 bits are needed to represent the four literals of the type MIDAS_VALUES. Also assignment-1 is then interpreted as the assignment of value "01" to ROY and assignment-2 is interpreted as the assignment of value "11" to ROY, which may or may not be what the designer intends to do.

Note that the literals 'U', 'X', and 'Z' cannot be used directly to signify the metalogical values since these literals can be used in more than one type declaration to mean different things, as the following example shows.

```
type LOGIC5 is ('U', 'X', '0', '1', 'Z');
type CARAT is ('B', 'H', 'A', 'S', 'K', 'E', 'R', 'U', 'X', 'Z', 'D');

signal SOG: LOGIC5;
signal MY_NAME: CARAT;

SOG <= 'X';
MY_NAME <= 'U';
```

In this example, how does the ArchSyn system figure out which are the metalogical values and which are not? The ENUM_TYPE_ENCODING attribute is again used to specify this. For example,

```
attribute ENUM_TYPE_ENCODING of LOGIC5: type is "U D 0 1 Z";
```

implies that signal SOG is of size 1 bit and that the signal assignment to SOG assigns a value of don't-care. Signal MY_NAME needs 4 bits for its representation and the signal assignment statement infers the assignment of the value "0111" to signal MY_NAME.

Metalogicals in type STD_ULOGIC

The type STD_ULOGIC is defined in the IEEE standard package STD_LOGIC_1164 as follows.

```
type STD_ULOGIC is ( 'U',      -- Uninitialized
                     'X',      -- Forcing unknown
                     '0',      -- Forcing 0
                     '1',      -- Forcing 1
                     'Z',      -- High impedance
                     'W',      -- Weak unknown
                     'L',      -- Weak 0
                     'H',      -- Weak 1
                     '-'       -- Don't care
                   );
```

Given the interpretations of the literals of the enumeration type STD_ULOGIC as specified in the above comments, how can this information be conveyed to a synthesis system?

One option is to build it into the synthesis system. For example, if a literal '-' appears in a VHDL model, a check is made to see if this literal belongs to the type STD_ULOGIC that comes from the package STD_LOGIC_1164 which resides in design library IEEE, then this literal is to be interpreted as a don't-care value for synthesis. This check is necessary since the literal '-' can be used in user-defined types as well.

An alternate way to specify the interpretations, as is done in the ArchSyn synthesis system, is by using the attribute ENUM_TYPE_ENCODING.

```
attribute ENUM_TYPE_ENCODING of STD_ULOGIC: type
  -- 'U'  'X'  '0'  '1'  'Z'  'W'  'L'  'H'  '-'
  is "U    D    0    1    Z    D    0    1    D";
```

Using this attribute specification, the synthesis system interprets the literals in type STD_ULOGIC as follows. The literal 'U' implies an unknown value, the literals 'X', 'W', '-' imply a don't-care value, literal 'Z' implies a high-impedance value, literals '0' and 'L' imply the logic-0 value, and literals '1' and 'H' imply the logic-1 value for synthesis.

2.5.5   Array types

A typical synthesis system, including the ArchSyn synthesis system, supports array types of one dimension, and an array of an array type. The basic element of an array must be of size one bit. Arrays represent an ordered collection of wires or flip-flops. Here is an example of an array of an array.

```
type RF_TYPE is array (NATURAL range <>) of BIT_VECTOR(0 to 7);
signal REG_FILE_A: RF_TYPE (5 downto 0);
```

Signal REG_FILE_A is an array of an array with the first dimension's index ranging from 5 down to 0, and the second ranging from 0 to 7. Each array element is of type BIT which is of size one bit.

Let us look at another example.

```
type LOGIC5 is ('U', 'X', '0', '1', 'Z');
type REG_TYPE is array (0 to 25) of LOGIC5;
variable REG_X: REG_TYPE;
```

The variable REG_X represents an array of an array, 26 elements in the first dimension, with each element representing 3 bits. Three bits are needed to represent a value in type LOGIC5. If the literals 'U', 'X', and 'Z' in type LOGIC5 were not intended to be actual values for synthesis but represented metalogical values, then it is necessary to specify an enumeration type encoding that identifies the metalogical values. Such an encoding is specified using the following attribute specification.

```
attribute ENUM_TYPE_ENCODING of LOGIC5: type is "U D 0 1 Z";
```

With this attribute specification present, variable REG_X becomes an array of only one dimension with its index ranging from 0 to 25. This is because the basic element type of the array is now only one bit wide (need to represent only '0' and '1' in type LOGIC5, the rest are metalogical values).

2.5.6   Signed and unsigned types

VHDL does not provide an explicit way to model signed and unsigned numbers. A limited capability is provided in VHDL in terms of integer types. An integer type can represent a signed number depending on whether the range contains a negative number. The disadvantage of using this type is that it is not possible to directly access each element of an object of an integer type.

An alternate approach is to define two new array types, SIGNED and UNSIGNED, that are similar to type BIT_VECTOR. These types are interpreted by a synthesis system as signed and unsigned numbers respectively. Here are the definitions for these types.

> **type** SIGNED **is array** (NATURAL **range** <>) **of** BIT;
> **type** UNSIGNED **is array** (NATURAL **range** <>) **of** BIT;

Notice that both types have the same definition as type BIT_VECTOR. The type SIGNED is interpreted as a signed number. Values are stored in two's complement form with the leftmost bit as the most significant bit. The type UNSIGNED is interpreted as an unsigned number. Notice that the conventions being followed for the above two types are the same as those being followed for the types discussed earlier, for example, the integer types and type BIT_VECTOR.

Having defined the two basic types, it becomes necessary to provide operator overloading functions on these two types. Conversion functions that convert between types SIGNED, UNSIGNED, BIT_VECTOR and integer types become necessary and useful. Shown below is a sample list of overloaded functions and conversion functions using these types.

> **function** "+" (L, R: SIGNED) **return** SIGNED;
> **function** "*" (L: SIGNED; R: UNSIGNED) **return** SIGNED;
> **function** "<" (L, R: SIGNED) **return** BOOLEAN;
>
> **function** TO_SIGNED (OPD: INTEGER; SIZE: NATURAL) **return** SIGNED;
> **function** TO_INTEGER (OPD: UNSIGNED) **return** INTEGER;

A synthesis system typically provides this capability to the user by providing a package containing these types and functions. The ArchSyn system provides a package called STD_LOGIC_ARITH. This package contains arithmetic operations and other utility functions defined on the SIGNED and UNSIGNED types. These types are based on the element type STD_LOGIC. The type STD_LOGIC is defined in the IEEE standard package STD_LOGIC_1164. The declaration for the SIGNED and UNSIGNED types that appear in package STD_LOGIC_ARITH are as follows.

> **type** SIGNED **is array** (NATURAL **range** <>) **of** STD_LOGIC;
> **type** UNSIGNED **is array** (NATURAL **range** <>) **of** STD_LOGIC;

Appendix B gives a listing of the package STD_LOGIC_ARITH. Most of the examples in this book are based on this package.

2.6   Resolution functions

A resolution function determines the effective value of a signal from the value of one or more of its drivers. In real hardware, there may or may not be logic associated with such a resolution function, since the effective value may be determined by the technology of the gates driving the signal. For synthesis purposes, one option would be to completely ignore the resolution function. However, the ArchSyn system provides an option that can be preset to indicate the type of resolution function to be used: wired-and, wired-or or tri-state. For example, if the option is set to wired-and, all the drivers for a signal are connected to an and gate and the output of this gate becomes the effective value for the signal.

Here is an example.

signal SAM: WIRED_OR BIT;
    -- WIRED_OR is the name of a resolution function.
. . .
SAM <= A **and** B;
SAM <= C **or** D;

Signal SAM has two drivers, one from each of the concurrent signal assignment statements. Therefore the signal SAM must have a resolution function associated with it so that an effective value for SAM can be computed. Figure 2-9 shows the logic that is represented by the above example.

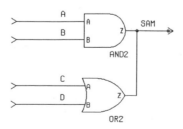

Figure 2-9 The drivers are shorted together.

However, resolution functions are not really synthesized since they represent technology-specific modeling. If such a model is synthesized using the ArchSyn system with the resolution function option set to wired-or, the logic shown in Figure 2-10 is generated. Note that an explicit or gate is generated to mimic the logic of the WIRED_OR function. Therefore, as far as synthesis is concerned, resolution functions have no impact or effect, that is, no logic is synthesized from the specified resolution function; additional and gates or or gates may be generated as appropriate based on the option specified.

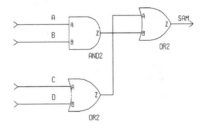

Figure 2-10 A logic gate does the resolution.

Types used in this book

The types used in all the examples in the rest of the book are based on the VHDL standard predefined types, the IEEE standard STD_LOGIC_1164 package and an arithmetic package STD_LOGIC_ARITH that is listed in Appendix B.

❏

Chapter 3

Mapping Statements to Gates

The previous chapter described the mapping from VHDL types and literals to hardware and the mapping from VHDL objects to hardware. This chapter describes the mapping of statements in VHDL to logic gates in hardware. It also explains how operators, expressions and assignments are mapped to hardware.

Sequential or combinational logic can be synthesized from a VHDL description. There are two main styles for describing combinational logic:

a. Using concurrent signal assignment statements: This is the most natural style, since it explicitly shows the parallelism in the hardware. It also implicitly shows the structure.

b. Using sequential statements in a process: This describes the sequential nature of a combinational logic model; this is because in simulation all statements in a process statement execute sequentially.

Synchronous logic elements, that is, flip-flops and latches, can be inferred by describing statements within a process in a certain style. It is best not to synthesize a memory as a two-dimensional array of flip-flops because this is an inefficient way to design a memory. The best way to create a memory is to instantiate a predefined memory block using a component instantiation statement.

3.1   Assignment statement

There are primarily two forms of an assignment statement:

- Signal assignment statement
- Variable assignment statement

Either of these represent, in hardware, logic that is derived from the expression on the right-hand-side of the assignment statement driving the signal or variable that appears on the left-hand-side of the assignment. Here are two examples.

```
signal STAT_OUT: STD_LOGIC;
STAT_OUT <= not STAT_IN;     -- Signal assignment statement.

variable PRESET, COUNT: UNSIGNED (0 to 3);
COUNT := PRESET + 1;          -- Variable assignment statement.
```

The first statement is a signal assignment statement that describes an inverter that has its input connected to a signal STAT_IN and whose output is STAT_OUT. See Figure 3-1. Delays, if any, specified in a signal assignment statement are usually ignored, as is the case in the ArchSyn synthesis system.

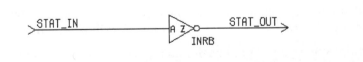

Figure 3-1 Combinational circuit from signal assignment statement.

The second statement is a variable assignment statement that describes an adder that takes PRESET and the integer 1 as inputs and places the result in the variable COUNT. Since the operator "+" is not predefined in VHDL to operate on the type UNSIGNED and on an integer type, it is assumed that such an overloaded "+" function exists. The synthesized circuit for the variable assignment statement is also shown in Figure 3-2.

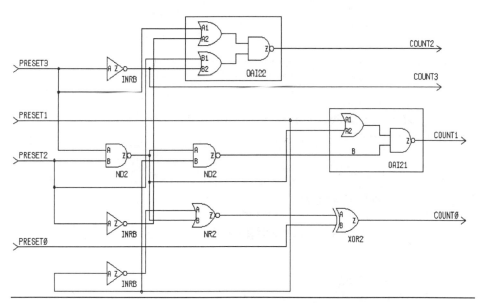

Figure 3-2 Combinational circuit from variable assignment statement.

The question of whether the target of the assignment is a wire, a flip-flop, or a latch, is decided by the context under which the assignment statement appears. For example, if the above signal assignment statement appeared, say, under the control of a clock as shown in the following example:

```
signal CLK, STAT_OUT: STD_LOGIC,
...
process (CLK)
begin
   if RISING_EDGE(CLK) then
      STAT_OUT <= not STAT_IN;      -- Signal assignment statement.
   end if;
end process;
```

then the target would be synthesized to be a flip-flop. This is shown in Figure 3-3.

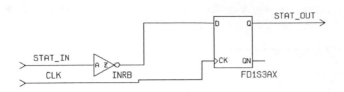

Figure 3-3 Target of an assignment is a flip-flop.

The more subtle differences between a variable assignment state-ment and a signal assignment statement are described later in the section on "Process statement".

3.2   *Logical operators*

Here is a model of a full-adder using concurrent signal assignment state-ments.

```
library IEEE;
use IEEE.STD_LOGIC_1164.all;
entity FULL_ADDER is
    port (A, B, CIN: in STD_LOGIC;
          SUM, COUT: out STD_LOGIC);
end;

architecture DATAFLOW of FULL_ADDER is
begin
    SUM <= (A xor B) xor CIN;
    COUT <= (A and B) or (B and CIN) or (A and CIN);
end;
```

The synthesized circuit is shown in Figure 3-4. The logical operators get directly mapped into primitive logic gates in hardware. Here is anoth-er example.

```
signal BI, STDY, TAP: BIT_VECTOR (0 to 3);
. . .
TAP <= BI xor STDY;
```

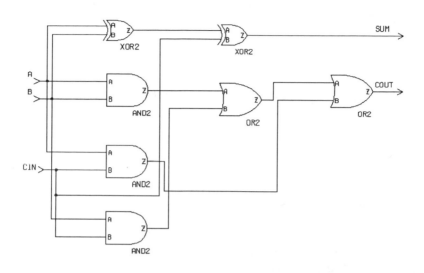

Figure 3-4 Logical operators map to primitive logic gates.

In this case, four exclusive-or gates are synthesized since each operand in the right-hand-side is of size 4. Figure 3-5 shows the synthesized circuit.

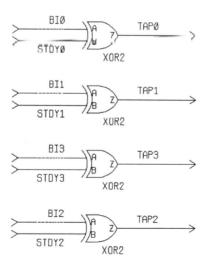

Figure 3-5 A bank of logic gates.

In the above examples, we see that there is a one-to-one correlation between a concurrent signal assignment statement and its synthesized logic. This is because a concurrent signal assignment implicitly shows the structure.

3.3   Arithmetic operators

When modeling arithmetic operators on vector operands, it is necessary to identify the number system being used to represent the operands. This may be achieved by providing a special package that defines the signed and unsigned arithmetic types, and the overloaded operator functions that operate on these types. A convention also needs to be established for representing the most significant bit.

In the ArchSyn synthesis system, two types, UNSIGNED and SIGNED, and their corresponding overloaded operator functions are defined in the package STD_LOGIC_ARITH. The rightmost bit is interpreted as the least significant bit. Vectors of type SIGNED represent values in the two's-complement form.

3.3.1   Unsigned arithmetic

Let us look at an example that uses an arithmetic operator on unsigned numbers.

```
library SYNTH;
use SYNTH.STD_LOGIC_ARITH.all;
entity UNSIGNED_ADDER is
    port (ARB, BET: in UNSIGNED (0 to 3);
        LOT: out UNSIGNED (0 to 3));
end UNSIGNED_ADDER;

architecture SIMPLE of UNSIGNED_ADDER is
begin
    LOT <= ARB + BET;
end SIMPLE;
```

In this example, we are trying to model a 4-bit adder. The number system for the operands is unsigned. This is determined by the type and the package used. The type UNSIGNED represents unsigned numbers with the leftmost bit as the most significant bit. The synthesized netlist for the entity UNSIGNED_ADDER is shown in Figure 3-6.

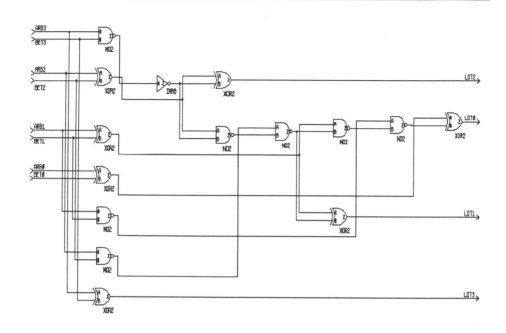

Figure 3-6 A 4-bit adder.

3.3.2   Signed arithmetic

Here is the same example as in the previous section, except that in this case, the operands are signed numbers. The type SIGNED defined in the package STD_LOGIC_ARITH represents signed numbers in the two's-complement form.

```
library SYNTH;
use SYNTH.STD_LOGIC_ARITH.all;
entity SIGNED_ADDER is
    port (ARB, BET: in SIGNED (0 to 3);
          LOT: out SIGNED (0 to 3));
end SIGNED_ADDER;

architecture SIMPLE of SIGNED_ADDER is
begin
    LOT <= ARB + BET;
end SIMPLE;
```

The synthesized netlist is the same as that for the entity UNSIGNED_ADDER since a "+" function behaves the same for unsigned numbers as well as for signed numbers that are in the two's-complement form. The difference is that the entity UNSIGNED_ADDER is capable of adding numbers in the range 0 through 15, while the entity SIGNED_ADDER has the capability of adding numbers in the range −8 to 7.

3.3.3   Computing result size

How is the length of a result of an arithmetic operator operating on vector operands computed? Assume L and R are the two input operands.

- + , − : Result size is the larger of L'LENGTH and R'LENGTH. For signed numbers, input operands are sign-extended to the larger of L'LENGTH and R'LENGTH before performing the appropriate operation. For unsigned numbers, operands are zero-extended.
- ∗ : Result size is L'LENGTH+R'LENGTH.
- / : Result size is L'LENGTH.
- **mod**, **rem**: Result size is R'LENGTH.
- − (unary), **abs**: Result size is same as input operand.

3.3.4   Modeling a carry

Note that the "+" and "−" operators return a size equal to the largest of its operands. In some cases, a "+" or a "−" operator can return a carry or a borrow respectively. The question is how can then a carry or a borrow be modeled? The trick is to provide an argument to the operator one bigger than the size of the operand. This can be achieved by using the concatenation operator. Here is such an example.

```
signal CDO_BUS: UNSIGNED (5 downto 0);
signal ONE_UP: UNSIGNED (6 downto 0);
. . .
ONE_UP <= ('0' & CDO_BUS ) + 1;
```

The size of the largest operand for the "+" operator is 7, the result of the operation is 7 bits and ONE_UP(6) has the carry bit.

3.4   Relational operators

Relational operators can be modeled similar to arithmetic operators. In this case, the logic produced from synthesis is different depending on whether unsigned or signed numbers are being compared. Again since the VHDL standard does not define relational operations on unsigned or signed vector operands, an arithmetic package needs to be used. Here is an example of a relational operator that is used with unsigned numbers. Figure 3-7 shows the synthesized netlist.

```
library SYNTH;
use SYNTH.STD_LOGIC_ARITH.all;
entity GT is
    port (A, B: in UNSIGNED (7 downto 0);
          Z: out BOOLEAN);
end GT;

architecture DF of GT is
begin
    Z <= A(3 downto 0) > B(7 downto 4);
end DF;
```

Here is an example that uses signed numbers. Note that in this case, we have to use the type SIGNED because values of type SIGNED represent signed numbers. Figure 3-8 shows the synthesized netlist.

```
library SYNTH;
use SYNTH.STD LOGIC_ARITH.all;
entity NE is
    port (A, B: in SIGNED (0 to 7);
          Z: out BOOLEAN);
end NE;

architecture DF of NE is
begin
    Z <= A /= B;          -- Z gets assigned the value of A not equals B.
end DF;
```

3.5   Vectors and slices

Operations using array vectors, slices and vector elements can be used in a model.

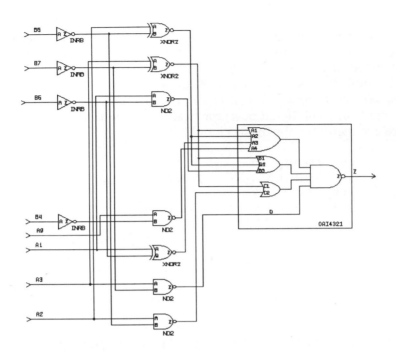

Figure 3-7 Unsigned ">" relational operator.

3.5.1   Constant index

Here is an example that uses constant values for array indices, slice and range indices.

```
library IEEE;
use IEEE.STD_LOGIC_1164.all;
package ARRAYS is
    type BANK is array (0 to 1) of STD_LOGIC_VECTOR (3 downto 0);
end ARRAYS;

library IEEE;
use IEEE.STD_LOGIC_1164.all, WORK.ARRAYS.all;
entity VECTORS is
    port (A, B, C: in STD_LOGIC_VECTOR (3 downto 0);
          REG_FILE: inout BANK;
          ZCAT: out STD_LOGIC_VECTOR (3 downto 0));
end VECTORS;
```

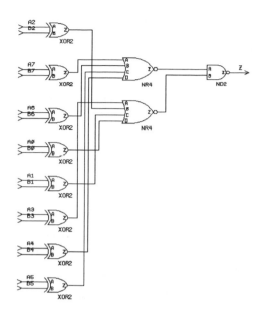

Figure 3-8 Signed "/=" relational operator.

architecture EXAMPLE **of** VECTORS **is**
begin
   ZCAT (3 **downto** 1) <= A(2) & C(3 **downto** 2);
   ZCAT(0) <= REG_FILE(1)(3);
   REG_FILE(0) <= A **and** B **or** C;
end EXAMPLE;

Note that REG_FILE is an inout port since the port is both read and written to. Figure 3-9 shows the synthesized netlist. The concatenation operator "&" is used to generate a bigger array. The example shows an element of an array of an array being read and assigned to an element of a one-dimensional array. Also an assignment is made to a vector of an array of an array.

3.5.2   Non-constant index

It is possible to use a non-constant as an index in an array element selection as shown in the following model.

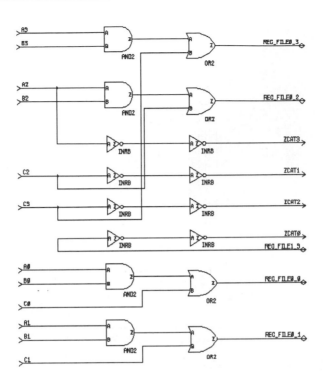

Figure 3-9 Vectors and slices.

```
library IEEE; use IEEE.STD_LOGIC_1164.all;
entity NON_COMPUTE_RIGHT is
   port (DATA: in STD_LOGIC_VECTOR(0 to 3);
         INDEX: in NATURAL range 0 to 3;
         DOUT: out STD_LOGIC);
end;


architecture EXAMPLE of NON_COMPUTE_RIGHT is
begin
   DOUT <= DATA (INDEX);
end;
```

In this case, a multiplexer is generated as shown in the synthesized netlist of Figure 3-10.

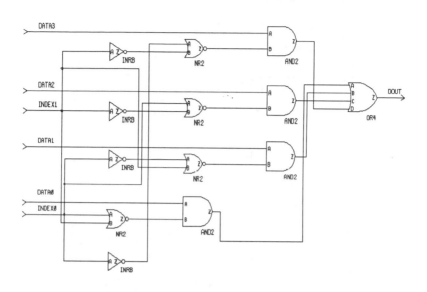

Figure 3-10 Non-constant index generates a multiplexer.

Here is another example of a non-constant index; this time it is used on the left-hand-side of an assignment. A decoder is synthesized for this behavior, as shown in Figure 3-11.

```
entity NON_COMPUTE_LEFT is
  port (MEM: out BIT_VECTOR (7 downto 0);
        STORE: in BIT;
        ADDR: in NATURAL range 0 to 7);
end NON_COMPUTE_LEFT;

architecture EXAMPLE of NON_COMPUTE_LEFT is
begin
  MEM(ADDR) <= STORE;
end EXAMPLE;
```

3.6 Process statement

A process statement is used to model the sequential behavior of a circuit. Here is an example of a process statement that contains variable assignment statements. Figure 3-12 shows the synthesized netlist.

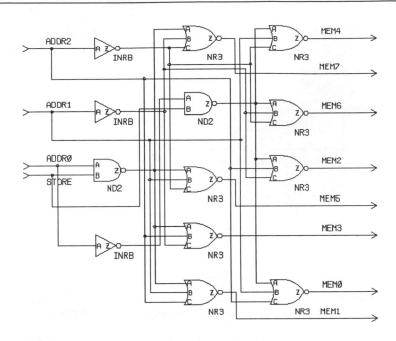

Figure 3-11 A decoder generated from a non-constant index.

```
entity PAR is
    port (A, B, C, D: in BIT;
          Z: out BIT);
end PAR;

architecture SEQ of PAR is
begin
    process (A, B, C, D)
        variable TEMP1, TEMP2: BIT;
    begin
        TEMP1 := A xor B;
        TEMP2 := C xor D;
        Z <= TEMP1 xor TEMP2;
    end process;
end SEQ;
```

Signals in a sensitivity list are usually ignored by a synthesis system; the ArchSyn synthesis system issues warnings about missing signals
in the sensitivity list. Consequently, the synthesized netlist may not
match the simulation semantics if all signals whose values are read in a

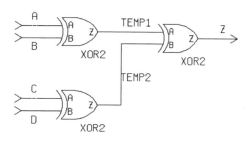

Figure 3-12 Variable assignment statements.

process do not appear in the sensitivity list of the process. More on this is discussed in Chapter 5.

A variable holds a temporary value and does not necessarily infer an unique wire in hardware as the following example shows.

```
VAR_EX: process (A, B, C)
    variable T1, T2: BIT;
begin
    T1 := A and B;
    T2 := T1 xor C;
    T1 := T2 nand A;
    Z <= T1 nor T2;
end process VAR_EX;
```

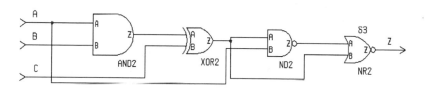

Figure 3-13 One variable can represent many wires.

In the synthesized netlist, shown in Figure 3-13, the output of the AND2 gate is the variable T1; so is the output of the ND2 gate. In the above example, each assignment to a variable infers a unique wire.

3.7   *If statement*

An `if` statement represents logic that is conditionally controlled. Here is an example.

```
if A > B then
   Z := A;
else
   Z := B;
end if;
```

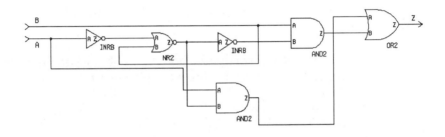

Figure 3-14 Logic derived from an `if` statement.

The logic corresponding to this `if` statement is shown in Figure 3-14. Here is another example of an `if` statement.

```
library IEEE;
use IEEE.STD_LOGIC_1164.all;
entity SIMPLE_ALU is
   port (CTRL: in BOOLEAN;
         A, B: in STD_LOGIC_VECTOR(0 to 3);
         Z: out STD_LOGIC_VECTOR(0 to 3));
end SIMPLE_ALU;

architecture EXAMPLE of SIMPLE_ALU is
begin
   process (CTRL, A, B)
   begin
      if CTRL then
         Z <= A and B;
      else
         Z <= A or B;
      end if;
```

        end process;
        end EXAMPLE;

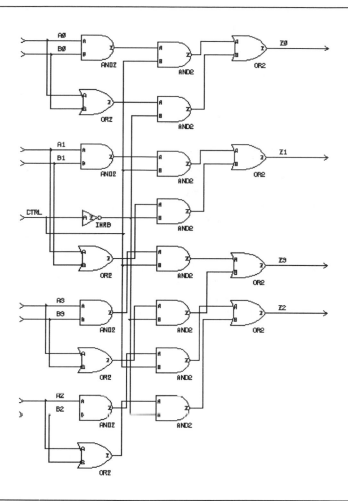

Figure 3-15 Conditional selection of operations.

The synthesized logic is shown in Figure 3-15.

3.7.1 Inferring latches from if statements

Consider the process statement in the following entity.

```
library SYNTH;
use SYNTH.STD_LOGIC_ARITH.all;
entity INCR is
  port (PHY: in BIT;
        Z: out UNSIGNED (0 to 1));
end;

architecture TEST of INCR is
begin
  INCR_L: process (PHY)
    variable ONES: UNSIGNED (0 to 1);
  begin
    if PHY = '1' then
      ONES := ONES + 1;
    end if;

    Z <= ONES;
  end process INCR_L;
end TEST;
```

The semantics for a process statement specifies that every time an event happens on signal PHY (denoted in the sensitivity list), the if statement executes and the variable ONES gets incremented. Between events on signal PHY, the value of ONES has to be saved; this is done using a latch, as shown in Figure 3-16.

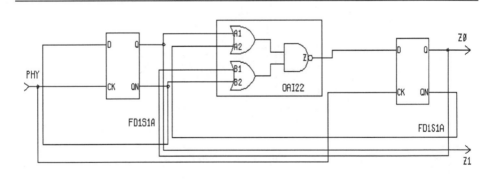

Figure 3-16 A variable is synthesized as a latch.

A general rule for latch inferencing is that if a variable declared in a process, or a signal, is not assigned in all branches of an if statement, then a latch is inferred. A variable declared in a subprogram never infers a latch since such a variable never retains its value through subsequent subprogram calls.

Let us now look at an example of a signal that is not assigned in all branches of an if statement.

```
package EXAM is
   type GRADE_TYPE is (FAIL, PASS, EXCELLENT);
end;

use WORK.EXAM.all;
entity COMPUTE is
   port (MARKS: in NATURAL range 0 to 10;
       GRADE: out GRADE_TYPE);
end;

architecture BIN of COMPUTE is
begin
   process (MARKS)
   begin
     if MARKS < 5 then
        GRADE <= FAIL;
     elsif MARKS >= 5 and MARKS < 7 then
        GRADE <= PASS;
     end if;
   end process;
end;
```

In this example, what should be the value of signal GRADE if MARKS has the value 8? It appears that the designer intends it to be a don't care, but from the simulation semantics viewpoint, the signal GRADE retains its last value, since no value is assigned to the signal explicitly when MARK has the value 8. Therefore a latch is inferred for the signal GRADE in keeping with the simulation semantics of a signal. The synthesized logic is shown in Figure 3-17.

If a signal or a variable is not assigned in all branches of an if statement and the intention is not to infer a latch, then the signal or variable must be assigned a value explicitly in all the branches of the if statement. If the previous example is modified by specifying the assignment to the signal in all branches, we get the following program.

```
package EXAM is
   type GRADE_TYPE is (FAIL, PASS, EXCELLENT);
end;
```

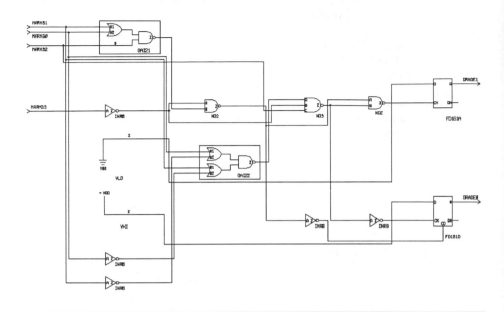

Figure 3-17 A signal is also inferred as a latch.

```
use WORK.EXAM.all;
entity COMPUTE_MOD is
   port (MARKS: in NATURAL range 0 to 10;
        GRADE: out GRADE_TYPE);
end;

architecture BIN of COMPUTE_MOD is
begin
   process (MARKS)
   begin
      if MARKS < 5 then
         GRADE <= FAIL;
      elsif MARKS >= 5 and MARKS < 7 then
         GRADE <= PASS;
      else
         GRADE <= EXCELLENT;
      end if;
   end process;
end;
```

In this case, signal GRADE is not a latch. Figure 3-18 shows the synthesized netlist.

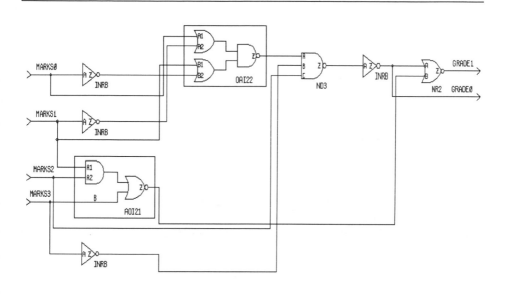

Figure 3-18 Signal GRADE is not a latch.

3.8 Case statement

Here is an example of a case statement.

```
package PACK_A is
   type OP_TYPE is (ADD, SUB, MUL, DIV);
end;

use WORK.PACK_A.all;
library SYNTH;
use SYNTH.STD_LOGIC_ARITH.all;
entity ALU is
   port (OP: in OP_TYPE;
         A, B: in UNSIGNED (0 to 1);
         Z: out UNSIGNED (0 to 1));
end ALU;

architecture SIMPLE of ALU is
begin
   process (OP, A, B)
   begin
```

```
case OP is
    when ADD =>
        Z <= A + B;
    when SUB =>
        Z <= A - B;
    when MUL =>
        Z <= A * B;
    when DIV =>
        Z <= A / B;
    end case;
  end process;
end;
```

A case statement behaves like a nested if statement, that is, the OP value is checked with the first case choice, if it does not match, the second case choice is checked and so on. The equivalent if statement for the above case statement is shown next.

```
if OP = ADD then
    Z <= A + B;
elsif OP = SUB then
    Z <= A - B;
elsif OP = MUL then
    Z <= A * B;
elsif OP = DIV then
    Z <= A / B;
end if;
```

The logic synthesized is shown in Figure 3-19. Note that an alternate way to generate logic is to generate a decoder for a case statement. The ArchSyn synthesis system does not produce such a decoder, but translates a case statement into its equivalent if statement for synthesis.

Here is another example of a case statement. The logic synthesized is shown in Figure 3-20.

```
package PAT is
    type WEEKDAY is (MON, TUE, WED, THU, FRI, SAT, SUN);
end PAT;

use WORK.PAT.all;
entity CASE_EX is
    port (DAY_OF_WORK: in WEEKDAY;
          SLEEP_TIME: out INTEGER range 0 to 15);
end CASE_EX;
```

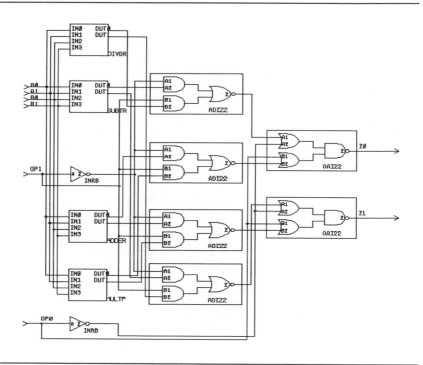

Figure 3-19 A 2-bit ALU.

```
architecture TEST of CASE_EX is
begin
  process (DAY_OF_WORK)
  begin
    case DAY_OF_WORK is
      when MON to THU =>
        SLEEP_TIME <= 6;
      when FRI =>
        SLEEP_TIME <= 8;
      when SAT =>
        SLEEP_TIME <= 9;
      when SUN =>
        SLEEP_TIME <= 7;
    end case;
  end process;
end architecture TEST;
```

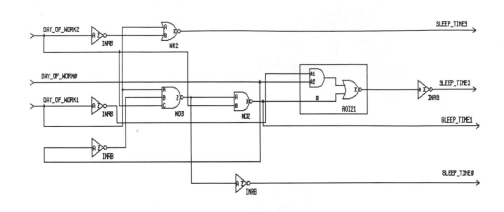

Figure 3-20 A case statement example.

3.8.1 Inferring latches from case statements

A latch can be inferred for a signal or a variable in a case statement, just like in an if statement. If a signal or a variable is not assigned a value in all possible branches of a case statement, a latch is inferred. See the following example.

```
package COLLECT is
   type STATES is (S0, S1, S2, S3);
end;

use WORK.COLLECT.all;
entity STATE_UPDATE is
   port (CURR_STATE: in STATES;
         Z: out INTEGER range 0 to 3);
end STATE_UPDATE;

architecture UPDATE of STATE_UPDATE is
begin
   process (CURR_STATE)
   begin
      case CURR_STATE is
         when S0 | S3 =>
            Z <= 0;
         when S1 =>
            Z <= 3;
         when others =>
            null;
```

> **end case**;
> **end process**;
> **end** UPDATE;

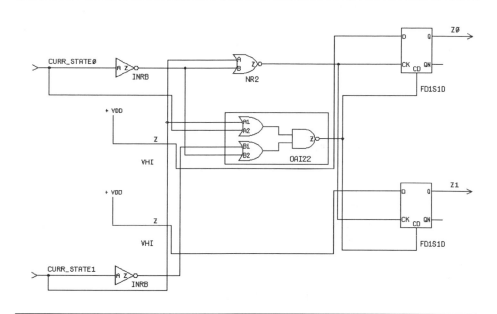

Figure 3-21 Latch inferred for a signal in a `case` statement.

The signal Z is not assigned a value for all possible values of the input signal CURR_STATE. Therefore in keeping with the simulation semantics of a signal, a latch is inferred for signal Z. The synthesized netlist that shows the latch is shown in Figure 3-21. In terms of latch inferencing, a `case` statement behaves identically to an `if` statement. If a latch is to be avoided, insert an initial value to signal Z before the `case` statement, as shown next. This assignment to Z causes it to be defined for all values of CURR_STATE.

```
. . .
process (CURR_STATE)
begin
    Z <= 0;          -- This statement added.

    case CURR_STATE is
    . . .
```

3.9   *Loop statement*

There are three kinds of loop statement in VHDL:

- while-loop
- for-loop
- loop

The for-loop statement is the one typically supported for synthesis, as in the ArchSyn synthesis system. The ArchSyn system implements a for-loop by unrolling the for-loop, that is, all statements within the for-loop are replicated, once for each value of the for-loop index. This puts a restriction on the for-loop parameters, which must therefore compute to constant values during synthesis. Here is an example of a for-loop statement.

```
library SYNTH;
use SYNTH.STD_LOGIC_ARITH.all;
entity DEMUX is
   port (A: in UNSIGNED (1 downto 0);
         Z: out UNSIGNED (3 downto 0));
end DEMUX;

architecture FOR_LOOP of DEMUX is
begin
   process (A)
      variable TEMP: INTEGER range 0 to 3;
   begin
      TEMP := TO_INTEGER (A);

      for J in Z'RANGE loop
         if TEMP = J then
            Z(J) <= '1';
         else
            Z(J) <= '0';
         end if;
      end loop;
   end process;
end;
```

The function TO_INTEGER converts an unsigned vector into an integer value; this function is present in the package STD_LOGIC_ARITH. When the for-loop is expanded, the following four if statements are obtained.

```
if TEMP = 3 then Z(3) <= '1'; else Z(3) <= '0'; end if;
if TEMP = 2 then Z(2) <= '1'; else Z(2) <= '0'; end if;
```

if TEMP = 1 **then** Z(1) <= '1'; **else** Z(1) <= '0'; **end if**;
if TEMP = 0 **then** Z(0) <= '1'; **else** Z(0) <= '0'; **end if**;

The synthesized logic is shown in Figure 3-22.

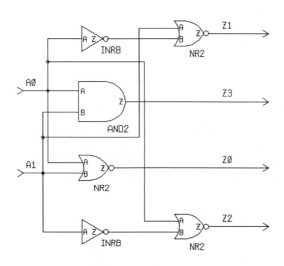

Figure 3-22 A for-loop example.

3.10 Null statement

A null statement means to do no action. Therefore no hardware logic is generated for this statement.

3.11 Wait statement

There are three basic forms of the wait statement:

wait for *time*;
wait until *condition*;
wait on *signal-list*;

The wait-until form is the one typically supported for synthesis. It is used in the ArchSyn synthesis system to imply synchronous logic behavior. If used, the `wait` statement must be the first statement in a process, and furthermore, the condition in the `wait` statement must be one of the allowed clock expressions that indicates a falling or a rising clock edge. The `wait` statement with the various forms of clock expressions that are allowed are:

> **wait until** *clock_name* = *clock_value*;
> **wait until** *clock_name* = *clock_value* **and** *clock_name*'EVENT;
> **wait until** *clock_name* = *clock_value* **and not** *clock_name*'STABLE;

where the *clock_value* is either a logic-0, which indicates a falling clock edge, or a logic-1, which indicates a rising clock edge. In addition, the following two forms can be used if the clock is of type STD_ULOGIC or of type STD_LOGIC; the functions RISING_EDGE and FALLING_EDGE are defined in the package STD_LOGIC_1164.

> **wait until** RISING_EDGE (*clock_name*);
> **wait until** FALLING_EDGE (*clock_name*);

Statements that follow a `wait` statement refer to statements that execute synchronously with the clock edge. A variable or a signal assigned a value following the `wait` statement is synthesized as a flip-flop. Here is an example.

```
library IEEE, SYNTH;
use IEEE.STD_LOGIC_1164.all, SYNTH.STD_LOGIC_ARITH.all;
entity INCREMENTOR is
   port (CLK: in STD_ULOGIC;
         COUNTER: buffer UNSIGNED (1 downto 0));
end INCREMENTOR;

architecture FLOP of INCREMENTOR is
begin
   process
   begin
      wait until CLK = '1';
      COUNTER <= COUNTER + 1;
   end process;
end FLOP;
```

The arithmetic package STD_LOGIC_ARITH needs to be included because a signal of type UNSIGNED is being added to an integer; the package contains the definition of the overloaded "+" operator and the

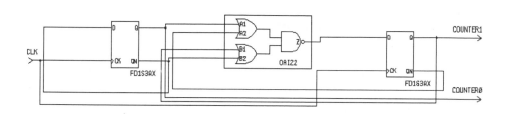

Figure 3-23 A wait statement implies synchronous logic.

definition of the type UNSIGNED. The logic in the process statement implies that every time signal CLK changes to a value '1', the counter is incremented. After synthesis, COUNTER is synthesized as two flip-flops with some additional combinational logic. The synthesized netlist is shown in Figure 3-23.

Any number of sequential statements can follow the wait statement; the wait statement must be the first and the only wait statement in a process. All variables and signals assigned within such a process are implemented as flip-flops. There is, however, a slight difference in the way they are implemented to match with the semantics of a signal or a variable. Let us look at another example.

```
signal SELFIRST: STD_ULOGIC;
. . .
SEQ: process
   variable RSHIFT: STD_ULOGIC;
begin
   wait until CK_A = '0';
   RSHIFT := RSHIFT and STROBE;
   SELFIRST <= RSHIFT or XFLAG;
   CHKSTOP <= SELFIRST xor MASK;
end process;
```

In the first variable assignment statement, the variable RSHIFT is being used before its definition; therefore the value of this variable needs to be saved in a flip-flop. The use of RSHIFT in the assignment statement implies that the right-hand-side expression in the first assignment statement (the logic at the D input of the RSHIFT flip-flop) is used as the value of RSHIFT in the second assignment statement. Signals SELFIRST and CHKSTOP are also constructed as flip-flops since they are assigned under the control of a clock. The use of SELFIRST in the last statement implies that the output of the flip-flop, that is, the old value of SELFIRST, is used.

This is because a signal is never assigned a value immediately but always after a certain delay. Thus, signal SELFIRST used in the last statement refers to the old value of SELFIRST and not to the value assigned in the previous statement.

Contrasting a signal assignment to a variable assignment, a variable gets assigned instantaneously in VHDL without any delays. RSHIFT is inferred as a flip-flop since it is used before its definition. Since RSHIFT is a variable, the input of the RSHIFT flip-flop (the current value of the variable) is used as the value of the operand in the second assignment statement. The synthesized netlist is shown in Figure 3-24.

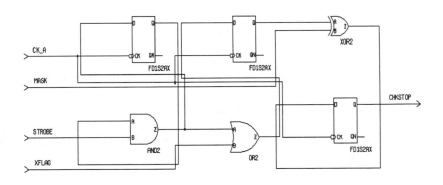

Figure 3-24 Variable vs. signal assignment following a `wait` statement.

Here is another example of a `wait` statement that is used to model an up-down counter.

```
library IEEE, SYNTH;
use IEEE.STD_LOGIC_1164.all, SYNTH.STD_LOGIC_ARITH.all;
entity UPDOWN is
    port (CTRL: in STD_LOGIC;
        CLK_B: in STD_LOGIC;
        COUT: out STD_LOGIC_VECTOR(1 downto 0));
end UPDOWN;

architecture WAIT_EX of UPDOWN is
    signal COUNTER: UNSIGNED (1 downto 0);
begin
    process
    begin
        wait until CLK_B = '0';
```

```
        if CTRL = '1' then
          COUNTER <= COUNTER + 1;
        else
          COUNTER <= COUNTER – 1;
        end if;
      end process;

      COUT <= STD_LOGIC_VECTOR (COUNTER); -- The right-hand-side of
                    -- the assignment is an example of a type conversion.
    end WAIT_EX;
```

The synthesized netlist is shown in Figure 3-25.

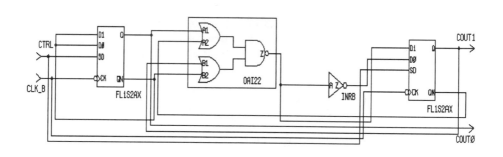

Figure 3-25 Up-down counter generated using a `wait` statement.

3.12 Modeling flip-flops

In the previous section, we saw how flip-flops can be inferred from signals and variables when they are assigned values within a process that contains a `wait` statement as the first statement. In the ArchSyn synthesis system, a flip-flop can also be inferred by using a special `if` statement in a process. The syntax is of the form:

```
    if clock-expression then
      sequential-statements
    end if;
```

where a *clock-expression* is one of the following:

RISING_EDGE (*clock_name*)
FALLING_EDGE (*clock_name*)
clock_name = clock_value **and** *clock_name*'EVENT
clock_name = clock_value **and** **not** *clock_name*'STABLE

where *clock_value* is either a logic-0 or a logic-1. The first two forms are allowed only if the clock is of type STD_ULOGIC or STD_LOGIC; the functions are defined in the package STD_LOGIC_1164.

A signal or a variable assigned in such an `if` statement is also inferred as a flip-flop. Here is an example.

```
library IEEE, SYNTH;
use IEEE.STD_LOGIC_1164.all, SYNTH.STD_LOGIC_ARITH.all;
entity COUNT4 is
   port (CLK, PRESET, UPDOWN: in STD_LOGIC;
         DATAIN: in UNSIGNED (1 downto 0);
         DOUT: out UNSIGNED (1 downto 0));
end COUNT4;

architecture EXAMPLE of COUNT4 is
   signal COUNTER: UNSIGNED (1 downto 0);
begin
   process (CLK, PRESET, UPDOWN, DATAIN)
   begin
     if RISING_EDGE (CLK) then
       if PRESET = '1' then
         COUNTER <= DATAIN;
       else
         if UPDOWN = '1' then
           COUNTER <= COUNTER + 1;
         else
           COUNTER <= COUNTER - 1;
         end if;
       end if;
     end if;

     DOUT <= COUNTER;
   end process;
end EXAMPLE;
```

In this example, signal COUNTER is assigned a value within a special `if` statement, thus inferring flip-flops. Notice that signal DOUT is not a flip-flop since it is assigned a value outside the `if` statement. The synthesized netlist for this model is shown in Figure 3-26.

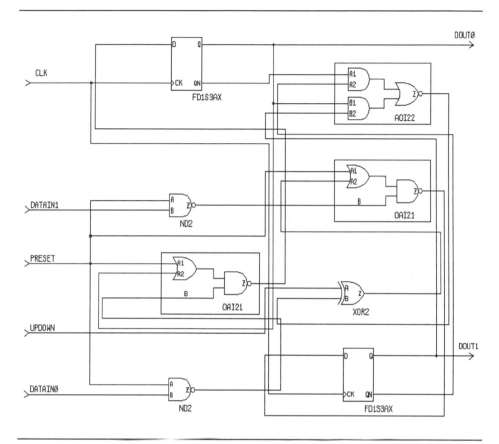

Figure 3-26 Modeling synchronous logic using an if statement.

The difference between the if statement style and the wait statement style is that in the if statement style more than one clock can be modeled in a single process. More importantly, the description of combinational logic and sequential logic can be lumped into one process. Using the wait statement style, logic associated with each clock has to be described in a different process, and synchronous logic has to be separated from combinational logic, with each having its own process statement.

Using the wait statement style, a design might be described using more than one process, such as the one shown in the following template.

```
process
begin
  wait until clock-expression-1;
  synchronous-logic-description-1
end process;

process
begin
  wait until clock-expression-2;
  synchronous-logic-description-2
end process;

process ( sensitivity-list )
begin
  combinational-logic-description
end process;
```

Using the if statement style, the same three processes can be merged into one single process, such as the one shown in the following template.

```
process ( sensitivity-list-with-clocks )
begin
  if clock-expression-1 then
    synchronous-logic-description-1
  end if;

  if clock-expression-2 then
    synchronous-logic-description-2
  end if;

  combinational-logic-description
end process;
```

3.12.1 Multiple clocks

Here is an example of multiple clocks used in a single model. The synthesized netlist is shown in Figure 3-27.

```
library IEEE;
use IEEE.STD_LOGIC_1164.all;
entity MULT_CLKS is
  port (VT15CK, ADDCLK, ADN,
        RESETN, SUB_CLR, SUBN,
        DS1CK: in STD_LOGIC;
        DS1_ADD, DS1_SUB: out STD_LOGIC);
```

```
  end;

architecture TEST of MULT_CLKS is
   signal ADD_STATE, SUB_STATE: STD_LOGIC;
begin
   process (VT15CK, DS1CK)
   begin
     if RISING_EDGE (VT15CK) then
        ADD_STATE <= ADDCLK nor (ADN or RESETN);
        SUB_STATE <= SUB_CLR xor (SUBN and RESETN);
     end if;

     if RISING_EDGE (DS1CK) then
        DS1_ADD <= ADD_STATE;
        DS1_SUB <= SUB_STATE;
     end if;
   end process;
end;
```

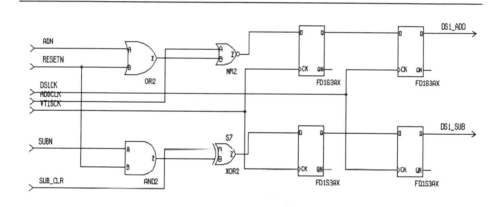

Figure 3-27 Multiple clocks within a process.

A typical restriction in this case is that a signal or a variable cannot be assigned under the control of more than one clock; this restriction also applies to the ArchSyn synthesis system.

3.12.2 Multi-phase clocks

Here is an example where two different phases of the same clock is used. Figure 3-28 shows the synthesized netlist.

```
library IEEE;
use IEEE.STD_LOGIC_1164.all;
entity MULTIPHASE_CLKS is
  port (CLK_A, A, B, C: in STD_LOGIC;
        E: out STD_LOGIC);
end;

architecture TEST of MULTIPHASE_CLKS is
  signal D: STD_LOGIC;
begin
  process (CLK_A)
  begin
    if RISING_EDGE (CLK_A) then
      E <= D and C;
    end if;

    if FALLING_EDGE (CLK_A) then
      D <= A and B;
    end if;
  end process;
end;
```

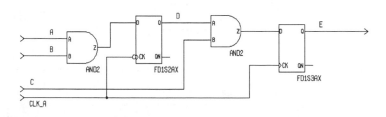

Figure 3-28 Different edges of the same clock within a process.

A typical restriction in this case is that a variable or a signal cannot be assigned under two different clock conditions or for that matter, under different clock edges; this restriction also applies to the ArchSyn synthesis system.

3.12.3 With asynchronous preset and clear

So far we have talked about simple D-type flip-flops. What if we wanted to infer a flip-flop with asynchronous preset and clear? To generate such a flip-flop, a special form of if statement has to be used. This is of the form:

```
if condition-1 then
    asynchronous-logic-1
elsif condition-2 then
    asynchronous-logic-2
elsif condition-3 then
    asynchronous-logic-3
-- Any number of elsif's
. . .
elsif clock-expression then
    synchronous-logic
end if;
```

The `if` statement may have one or more `elsif`'s but must not have any `else` clause. The last `elsif` clause must have a valid clock expression as its condition. A valid clock expression is of the form:

```
RISING_EDGE (clock_name)
FALLING_EDGE (clock_name)
clock_name = clock_value and clock_name'EVENT
clock_name = clock_value and not clock_name'STABLE
```

where *clock_value* is either a logic-0 or a logic-1. The logic in the last `elsif` clause describes synchronous logic. All other `elsif` branches describe asynchronous logic.

If a signal is assigned a value in any of the asynchronous sections and is also assigned in the synchronous part, that signal will get synthesized as a flip-flop with asynchronous preset and or clear. Depending on the value being assigned, the flip-flop could either be a flip-flop with asynchronous preset (if a non-zero value is assigned), or a flip-flop with asynchronous clear (if a zero value is being assigned), or a flip-flop with both.

Here is an example of an up-down counter with asynchronous preset and clear. The synthesized netlist is shown in Figure 3-29.

```
library IEEE, SYNTH;
use IEEE.STD_LOGIC_1164.all, SYNTH.STD_LOGIC_ARITH.all;
entity ASYNC_COUNT2 is
    port (CLK, PRESET, UPDOWN, CLEAR: in STD_LOGIC;
          DIN: in STD_LOGIC_VECTOR (1 downto 0);
          DOUT: out STD_LOGIC_VECTOR (1 downto 0));
end;

architecture EXAMPLE of ASYNC_COUNT2 is
    signal COUNTER: UNSIGNED (1 downto 0);
```

```
begin
  process (CLK, PRESET, UPDOWN, DIN, CLEAR, COUNTER)
  begin
    if PRESET = '1' then
      COUNTER <= UNSIGNED (DIN);
    elsif CLEAR = '1' then
      COUNTER <= (others => '0');
    elsif CLK = '1' and CLK'EVENT then
      if UPDOWN = '1' then
        COUNTER <= COUNTER + 1;
      else
        COUNTER <= COUNTER - 1;
      end if;
    end if;

    DOUT <= STD_LOGIC_VECTOR(COUNTER);
  end process;
end;
```

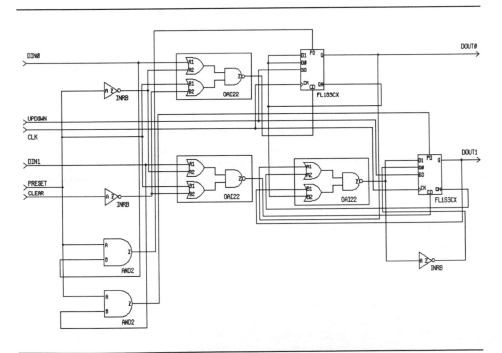

Figure 3-29 Flip-flops with asynchronous preset and clear.

3.12.4 With synchronous preset and clear

What if we want to model a flip-flop with synchronous preset and clear? Let us first examine the following process statement.

```
library IEEE, SYNTH;
use IEEE.STD_LOGIC_1164.all, SYNTH.STD_LOGIC_ARITH.all;
entity PRESET_COUNTER is
    port (CLK, PRESET, UPDOWN: in STD_LOGIC;
          DIN: in UNSIGNED (0 to 1);
          DOUT: out UNSIGNED(0 to 1));
end;


architecture IS_IT_SYNC_FF of PRESET_COUNTER is
    signal COUNTER: UNSIGNED (0 to 1);
begin
  process
  begin
    wait until CLK = '0';

    if PRESET = '1' then
      COUNTER <= DIN;
    else
      if UPDOWN = '1' then
        COUNTER <= COUNTER + 1;
      else
        COUNTER <= COUNTER - 1;
      end if;
    end if;
  end process;

    DOUT <= COUNTER;
end;
```

The synthesized netlist is shown in Figure 3-30. Notice that even though the synthesized logic behaves as specified, the flip-flop selected is a normal D-type flip-flop. The preset logic gets tied into the D-input of the flip-flop; this might potentially affect the critical path delay. This may not be what the designer intended.

To infer a flip-flop with preset and clear, a specially-provided procedure call, such as the procedure PRESET_CLEAR in the ArchSyn synthesis system, has to be used. If such a procedure call is used in the above process statement, the call provides a directive to the synthesis system to select a flip-flop with synchronous preset for signal COUNTER. The modi-

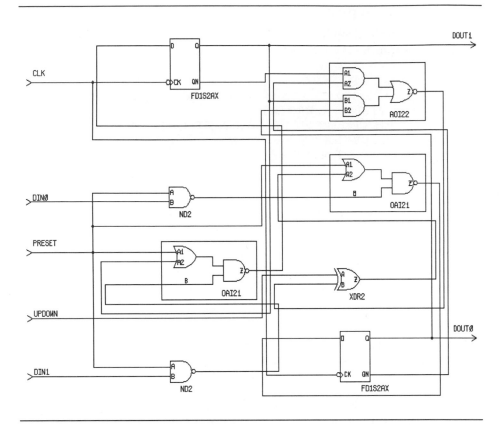

Figure 3-30 Synchronous preset and clear synthesized as combinational logic.

fied process statement with the procedure call is shown next. The synthesized netlist is shown in Figure 3-31.

```
PRE_CLR: process
begin
  wait until CLK = '0';

  if PRESET = '1' then
    PRESET_CLEAR (COUNTER, DIN);
  else
    if UPDOWN = '1' then
      COUNTER <= COUNTER + 1;
    else
      COUNTER <= COUNTER – 1;
    end if;
```

end if;
end process;

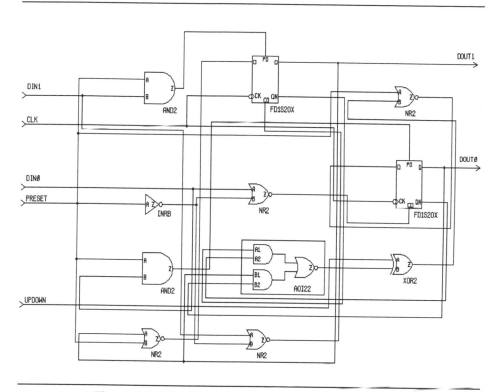

Figure 3-31 Flip-flops with synchronous preset and clear.

3.13 Modeling latches

In examples shown earlier using an `if` and a `case` statement, we saw how latches can be inferred when a signal or a variable is not assigned in all possible branches. This can sometimes be very confusing and may not be intended. To alleviate this problem, the ArchSyn synthesis system provides for an explicit way to model latches. This is done by using another special form of clock expression in an `if` statement that is of the form:

> **if** *clock-expression* **then**
>   *level-sensitive-synchronous-logic*
> **end if**;

where *clock-expression* is one of the following functions:

1. HIGH_LEVEL : implies logic-1 level control
2. LOW_LEVEL : implies logic-0 level control

If the clock expression is a call to the function HIGH_LEVEL, then all signals and variables assigned in the synchronous logic section part are implemented as latches with a positive level control; similarly for the function LOW_LEVEL. These two functions are defined in the STD_LOGIC_ARITH package. The clock expression provides a means of explicitly defining the latch enable.

Here is an example. The synthesized netlist is shown in Figure 3-32.

```
library IEEE, SYNTH;
use IEEE.STD_LOGIC_1164.all, SYNTH.STD_LOGIC_ARITH.all;
entity LATCHED_ALU is
   port (A, B: in SIGNED(0 to 4);
         CLK: in STD_LOGIC;
         Z: out SIGNED(0 to 4));
end;

architecture EXAMPLE of LATCHED_ALU is
begin
   process (CLK, A, B)
   begin
     if HIGH_LEVEL(CLK) then
        Z <= A nor B;
     end if;
   end process;
end;
```

3.14 Other forms of signal assignment

3.14.1 Conditional signal assignment statement

In VHDL, a conditional signal assignment statement has an equivalent process statement with an `if` statement in it. The ArchSyn synthesis system also transforms a conditional signal assignment statement to its equivalent process statement, which is then synthesized. Here is an example.

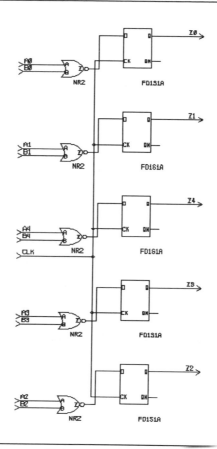

Figure 3-32 Level-sensitive latches.

```
architecture TEST of COND_ASSIGN is
begin
    STOP_XM <= START_XM xor SHIFT_VAL when RESET = '0'
                  else START_XM or SHIFT_VAL;
end;
```

The equivalent process for the assignment statement is shown next, and the synthesized netlist is shown in Figure 3-33.

```
process (RESET, START_XM, SHIFT_VAL)
begin
    if RESET = '0' then
        STOP_XM <= START_XM xor SHIFT_VAL;
    else
```

```
        STOP_XM <= START_XM or SHIFT_VAL;
    end if;
end process;
```

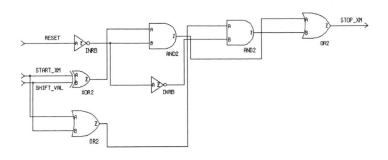

Figure 3-33 Logic generated from a conditional signal assignment statement.

3.14.2 Selected signal assignment statement

In VHDL, a selected signal assignment statement is equivalent to a process statement with a case statement in it. The ArchSyn synthesis system transforms a selected signal assignment to its equivalent process and then synthesizes the process statement. Here is an example.

```
package P1 is
    type STATES is (RESET, WAITS, APPLY, DONE);
end;

use WORK.P1.all;
entity SEL_ASSIGN is
    port (CURR_STATE: in STATES;
          RFLAG: out BIT_VECTOR(0 to 1));
end;

architecture TEST of SEL_ASSIGN is
    signal CURR_STATE: STATES;
begin
    with CURR_STATE select
        RFLAG <=  "00" when RESET | WAITS,
                  "10" when APPLY,
                  "11" when others;
end;
```

The equivalent process statement with a case statement in it is shown next and the synthesized netlist is shown in Figure 3-34.

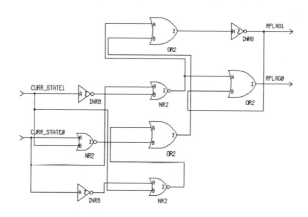

Figure 3-34 Logic generated from a selected signal assignment statement.

```
process (CURR_STATE)
begin
  case CURR_STATE is
    when RESET | WAITS =>
      RFLAG <= "00";
    when APPLY =>
      RFLAG <= "10";
    when others =>
      RFLAG <= "11";
  end case;
end process;
```

3.14.3 Sequential signal assignment statement

Here is an example of a process statement with some sequential signal assignment statements.

```
entity SEQ_SIG is
  port (MERGE: in BOOLEAN;
        ER, XMT, FDDI: in BIT;
        CLAIM: out BIT);
end SEQ_SIG;

architecture TEST of SEQ_SIG is
  signal FCR: BIT;
begin
```

```
          process (MERGE, ER, XMT, FDDI)
          begin
             FCR <= ER or XMT;                -- Assignment 1.

             if MERGE then
                CLAIM <= FCR and FDDI;         -- Assignment 2.
             else
                CLAIM <= FDDI;
             end if;
          end process;
       end;
```

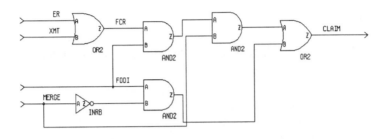

Figure 3-35 Signal assignments within a process.

There are three signal assignment statements in this example. Statements within a process statement execute sequentially. However, a signal is always assigned a value after a certain delay. Therefore the use of FCR in assignment 2 is the old value of FCR and not the value assigned in assignment 1. Most synthesis systems, however, ignore the delay in the signal assignment and the logic produced is as if the value assigned in assignment 1 is used in assignment 2. Note that simulation semantics may be different since signal FCR is not in the sensitivity list. To make the simulation results match between pre-synthesis and post-synthesis, the signal FCR must also appear in the sensitivity list so that when the value of FCR changes, the simulator executes the process a second time. The synthesized netlist is shown in Figure 3-35.

Now let us look at the same case when a wait statement is introduced as the first statement in the process. Such an example is shown next.

```
architecture TEST of SEQ_SIG_FF is
  signal FCR: BIT;
begin
  process
  begin
    wait until CK = '1';
    FCR <= ER or XMT;              -- Assignment 1.

    if MERGE then
        CLAIM <= FCR and FDDI;     -- Assignment 2.
    else
        CLAIM <= FDDI;
    end if;
  end process;
end;
```

In this case, the sequential statements infer synchronous logic. Signals FCR and CLAIM both infer flip-flops. Usage of signal FCR in assignment 2 now refers to the output of the flip-flop FCR, that is, the old value, rather than the value assigned in assignment 1. Simulation results between behavior and synthesized netlist now match. The synthesized netlist for this example in shown in Figure 3-36.

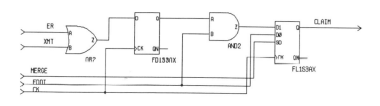

Figure 3-36 Signal assignments following a `wait` statement.

3.15 *Functions*

A function call represents combinational logic since a function call is always part of an expression in VHDL. A function call is synthesized by the ArchSyn synthesis system by expanding the function call into inline code. Any local variable declared within the function is treated as a pure temporary, in keeping with the simulation semantics of a variable declared within a subprogram; such a variable gets synthesized as a wire. Here is an example of a function call.

```
entity FUNC_CALL is
    port (XBC: out BOOLEAN;
          DATAIN: in BIT_VECTOR(0 to 5));
end;

architecture EXAMPLE of FUNC_CALL is
    function ODD_ONES (A: BIT_VECTOR) return BOOLEAN is
        variable RESULT: BIT;
    begin
      RESULT := '0';

      for K in A'RANGE loop
        RESULT := RESULT xor A(K);
      end loop;

      if RESULT = '0' then
        return FALSE;
      else
         return TRUE;
      end if;
    end ODD_ONES;
begin
    XBC <= ODD_ONES (DATAIN);
end;
```

After in-line expansion of the function call and further in-line expansion of the for-loop statement, we get the following code.

```
RESULT := '0';
RESULT := RESULT xor DATAIN(0);
RESULT := RESULT xor DATAIN(1);
RESULT := RESULT xor DATAIN(2);
RESULT := RESULT xor DATAIN(3);
RESULT := RESULT xor DATAIN(4);
RESULT := RESULT xor DATAIN(5);
XBC <= RESULT;
```

The synthesized netlist is shown in Figure 3-37. Note that a variable defined within a function can never be synthesized as a latch since the value of a variable defined in a function is never saved between subsequent function calls.

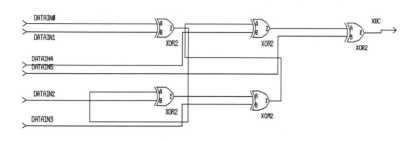

Figure 3-37 A function call example.

3.16 Procedures

A procedure call can represent either combinational logic or sequential logic depending on the context under which the procedure call occurs. By this, we mean that the output parameters of a procedure call may imply memory depending on the context in which they are assigned. For example, if a procedure call occurs in a process statement with a `wait` statement as the first statement, then any signal output parameter in a procedure call is synthesized as a flip-flop. Here is an example of a procedure call that represents pure combinational logic.

```
library IEEE;
use IEEE.STD_LOGIC_1164.all;
entity PROC_CALL is
    port (SHA, SHB: in STD_LOGIC_VECTOR(0 to 3);
          SHCARR: in STD_LOGIC;
          SHSUM: out STD_LOGIC_VECTOR(0 to 3);
          SHCARROUT: out STD_LOGIC);
end;

architecture EXAMPLE of PROC_CALL is
    procedure ADD (A, B, CIN: in STD_LOGIC;
                     COUT, SUM: out STD_LOGIC) is
    begin
        SUM := A xor B xor CIN;
        COUT := A and B and CIN;
    end;
begin
```

```
process
   variable TCARR: STD_LOGIC_VECTOR (0 to 4);
   variable TSUM: STD_LOGIC_VECTOR (0 to 3);
begin
   TCARR(0) := SHCARR;

   for J in SHA'RANGE loop
      ADD (SHA(J), SHB(J), TCARR(J), TSUM(J), TCARR(J+1));
   end loop;

   SHCARROUT <= TCARR(4);
   SHSUM <= TSUM;
end process;
end;
```

After in-line expansion of the procedure call and the for-loop statement, we get the following code.

```
TCARR(0) := SHCARR;
TSUM(0) := SHA(0) xor SHB(0) xor TCARR(0);
TCARR(1) := SHA(0) and SHB(0) and TCARR(0);
TSUM(1) := SHA(1) xor SHB(1) xor TCARR(1);
TCARR(2) := SHA(1) and SHB(1) and TCARR(1);
TSUM(2) := SHA(2) xor SHB(2) xor TCARR(2);
TCARR(3) := SHA(2) and SHB(2) and TCARR(2);
TSUM(3) := SHA(3) xor SHB(3) xor TARR(3);
TCARR(4) := SHA(3) and SHB(3) and TCARR(3);
SHCARROUT <= TCARR(4);
SHSUM <= TSUM;
```

The synthesized logic is shown in Figure 3-38. Next is an example of a procedure call that is called under the control of a clock edge.

```
library IEEE;
use IEEE.STD_LOGIC_1164.all;
entity PROC_CALL_2 is
   port (BYTEREC: in STD_LOGIC_VECTOR (3 downto 0);
         CLK_FA: in STD_LOGIC;
         RFIF: out STD_LOGIC);
end;

architecture EXAMPLE of PROC_CALL_2 is
   procedure AND_BITS (A: in STD_LOGIC_VECTOR;
                signal Z: out STD_LOGIC) is
      variable RES: STD_LOGIC;
   begin
```

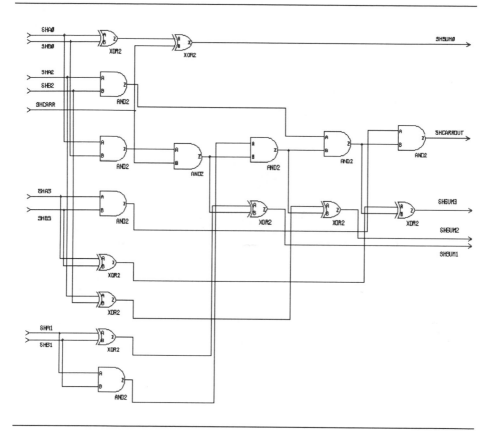

Figure 3-38 A procedure call example.

```
    RES := '1';

    for J in A'RANGE loop
      RES := RES and A(J);
    end loop;

    Z <= RES;
  end;
begin
  process
  begin
    wait until FALLING_EDGE(CLK_FA);
    AND_BITS (BYTEREC, RFIF);
  end process;
end;
```

In this example, signal RFIF is assigned a value under the control of clock CLK_FA; thus, signal RFIF gets synthesized as a flip-flop. The code after in-line expansion of the procedure call looks like this:

```
RES := '1';
RES := RES and BYTEREC(3);
RES := RES and BYTEREC(2);
RES := RES and BYTEREC(1);
RES := RES and BYTEREC(0);
RFIF <= RES;
```

The synthesized netlist is shown in Figure 3-39.

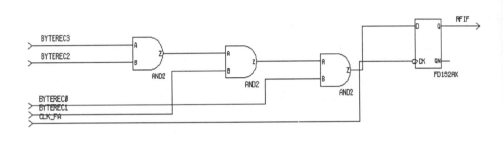

Figure 3-39 A procedure call following a `wait` statement.

3.17 Records

Here is an example that uses a record type.

```
package PACK is
    type STATES is (XMIT, RCV, INIT, DONE);
    type PACKET is
        record
            PACKET_ID: INTEGER range 0 to 3;
            PACKET_STATE: STATES;
        end record;
end;

use WORK.PACK.all;
entity INIT_PACKET is
    port (TSQ: out PACKET;
            SEND, CLK: in BIT);
```

```
    end;

    architecture RECORD_EXAMPLE of INIT_PACKET is
    begin
      process
        variable PACK_INDEX: NATURAL;
      begin
        wait until CLK = '1';

        if SEND = '1' then
          PACK_INDEX := (PACK_INDEX + 1) mod 4;
          TSQ.PACKET_ID <= PACK_INDEX;
          TSQ.PACKET_STATE <= INIT;
        end if;
      end process;
    end;
```

A record is split up into its individual elements for synthesis. Thus, for packet TSQ, the ArchSyn synthesis system treats this as two output ports, TSQ.PACKET_ID and TSQ.PACKET_STATE. Figure 3-40 shows the synthesized netlist for the above example.

3.18 Block statement

A block statement can be used to specify a guard, to limit signal scope and to partition a design as blocks. The ArchSyn synthesis system does not support block statements that specify a guard expression. A block statement does not cause any semantics or logic changes to occur, other than to limit the scope of signals declared within it. Here is an example.

```
    entity BLOCK_STMT is
      port (CIN, DIN: in BIT;
            REC_OUT: out BIT);
    end;

    architecture NESTED of BLOCK_STMT is
      signal STAT: BIT;
    begin
      B1: block
        signal STAT: BIT;
      begin
        STAT <= CIN and DIN;           -- Refers to STAT declared in block B1.
        NESTED.STAT <= CIN or DIN; -- Refers to STAT declared
                                   -- in architecture NESTED.
```

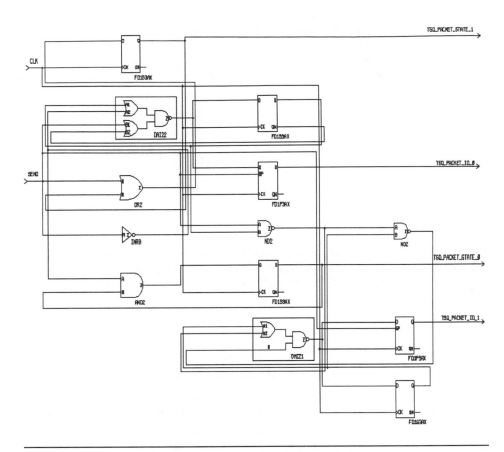

Figure 3-40 An example using a record type.

```
B2: block
   signal STAT: BIT;
begin
   STAT <= B1.STAT xor NESTED.STAT;
   REC_OUT <= B2.STAT; -- Alternately, refer simply as STAT.
   end block B2;
 end block B1;
end NESTED;
```

Figure 3-41 shows the synthesized netlist.

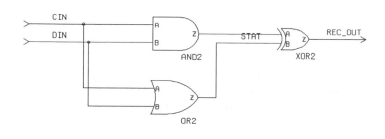

Figure 3-41 A block statement example.

3.19 Using metalogical values

In the previous chapter, we described the three metalogical values: don't-care, unknown, and high-impedance. These are specified in an encoding scheme using the attribute ENUM_TYPE_ENCODING with the values D, U, and Z. Because of their restrictive interpretation, each metalogical value has certain constraints with its usage. In this section, we specify the domain under which these metalogical values can be used and their interpretations as it applies to the ArchSyn synthesis system.

3.19.1 The don't-care value (D)

A don't-care value can be assigned to any signal or variable. The ArchSyn synthesis system intelligently selects either a logic-0 or a logic-1 value that can lead to minimal logic.

A don't-care value can be compared using the "=" (equality) operator or the "/=" (inequality) operator in an if statement. In such a case, the "=" operator always returns false while the "/=" operator always returns true. Here are some examples.

-- Assume that literal 'D' is encoded as the metalogical don't-care value.

RESET <= 'D';   -- Assign a don't-care value to signal RESET.
  -- Synthesis system will automatically select logic-0 or logic-1.

if SELECT = "DDDD" **then** -- The if condition always evaluates to false.
  . . .

elsif BSQ /= "DDD" **then**   -- `elsif` condition always evaluates to true.
. . .

3.19.2 The unknown value (U)

The unknown metalogical value cannot be used in an expression on the right-hand-side of an assignment. However it can be used with the "=" (equality) and the "/=" (inequality) operator in an `if` statement.

-- Assume literal 'U' is encoded to represent the metalogical unknown value.

if SAM /= "UUUUU" **then**   -- The `if` condition always evaluates to true.
. . .

if BAR = 'U' **then**   -- The `if` condition always evaluates to false.
. . .

3.19.3 The high-impedance value (Z)

The high-impedance value is used to generate a tri-state gate. A high-impedance value can be assigned to a signal or a variable; however, such an assignment must occur under the control of a condition, either in an `if` statement, or in a `case` statement. Here is an example.

```
library IEEE;
use IEEE.STD_LOGIC_1164.all;
entity TRI_STATE is
   port (RDY: in BOOLEAN;
         DINA, DINB: in STD_LOGIC;
         SEL1: out STD_LOGIC);
end TRI_STATE;

architecture EXAMPLE of TRI_STATE is
begin
   process (RDY, DINA, DINB)
   begin
      if RDY then
         SEL1 <= 'Z';  -- Literal 'Z' is encoded as a high-impedance
                       -- metalogical value in package STD_LOGIC_1164 using
                       -- the attribute ENUM_TYPE_ENCODING.
      else
         SEL1 <= DINA and DINB;
      end if;
   end process;
end EXAMPLE;
```

Figure 3-42 shows the synthesized netlist.

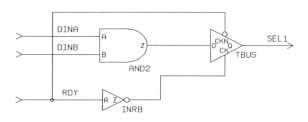

Figure 3-42 A high-impedance value produces a tri-state gate.

Furthermore, a high-impedance value can be compared using the "=" (equality) and the "/=" (inequality) operator in an if statement. The "=" operator always returns false while the "/=" operator always returns true. Here is an example.

```
-- Assume literal 'Z' is encoded as a high-impedance metalogical value.
if DACK /= "ZZZ" then        -- The if condition always evaluates to true.
   . . .
```

3.20 Component instantiation statement

A component instantiation statement can be written within an architecture body. The ArchSyn synthesis system simply treats such a component as a black box and does no further action, that is, the component appears in the synthesized netlist as if it were a primitive component. Here is an example of a full-adder entity that contains one component instantiation statement. Notice that in the synthesized netlist, shown in Figure 3-43, the MY_XOR block appears as it is described in the architecture body.

```
entity FA_MIX is
   port (A, B, CIN: in BIT;
         SUM, COUT: out BIT);
end FA_MIX;

architecture MIXED of FA_MIX is
   component MY_XOR
      port (IN0, IN1: in BIT;
            OUT0: out BIT);
```

```
        end component;

        signal SFT: BIT;
    begin
        X1: MY_XOR port map (IN0 => A, IN1 => B, OUT0 => SFT);

        COUT <= A and B and CIN;
        SUM <= SFT xor CIN;
    end MIXED;
```

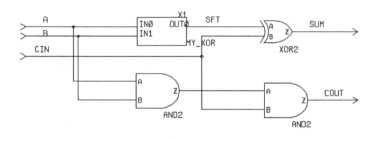

Figure 3-43 A component instance mixed with behavior.

3.21 Using predefined blocks

Component instantiation statements are often used when a designer is not satisfied with the quality of circuits produced by a synthesis tool. A designer may also have a library of predefined blocks such as memories. In such a case, the designer may prefer to instantiate a predefined block using a component instantiation statement instead of writing a behavioral description for the block. Thus a component instantiation statement provides flexibility in controlling the logic that is synthesized, and allows mixing of one or more predefined blocks as well.

Instantiating user-built multipliers

As a first example, consider the case where a designer is not happy with the multiplication logic generated by a synthesis tool. This logic might have been generated from the following code.

```
library IEEE, SYNTH;
use IEEE.STD_LOGIC_1164.all, SYNTH.STD_LOGIC_ARITH.all;
entity MULT_RED is
  port (A, B: in UNSIGNED(1 downto 0);
        Z: out STD_LOGIC);
end MULT_RED;

architecture EXAMPLE of MULT_RED is
  signal TEST: UNSIGNED (3 downto 0);
begin
  TEST <= A * B;              -- Multiply.
  Z <= TEST(0) and TEST(1) and TEST(2) and TEST(3);
end EXAMPLE;
```

In this example, the designer may instantiate a predefined multiplier as follows.

```
architecture OWN_INST of MULT_RED is
  component MY_MULT
    port (L, M: in UNSIGNED;
          P: out UNSIGNED);
  end component;

  signal TEST: UNSIGNED (3 downto 0);
begin
  M1: MY_MULT port map (L => A, M => B, P => TEST);
  Z <= TEST(0) and TEST(1) and TEST(2) and TEST(3);
end;
```

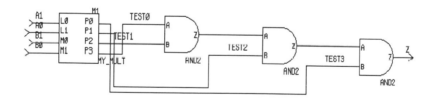

Figure 3-44 Instantiating a predefined multiplier.

The synthesized netlist for this example is shown in Figure 3-44. The designer may now use the predefined multiplier in the block MY_MULT.

Instantiating user-specific flip-flops

A flip-flop is yet another case where a designer may want to control the type of flip-flop being generated. Normally a flip-flop is inferred for a signal or a variable that is assigned a value within a process that has a special `wait` statement or a special `if` statement. However, such a synthesized flip-flop may not be optimal for the designer. A designer may want to use a custom-made flip-flop instead of the flip-flop generated by the synthesis tool. This can be modeled again by instantiating the predefined flip-flop as a component. Here is an example.

```
component MY_FF
    port (IN0, IN1: in STD_ULOGIC;
         OUT0: out STD_ULOGIC);
end component;
. . .
F1: MY_FF port map (IN0 => REQ, IN1 => DCK, OUT0 => NREQ);
-- The component instantiation statement replaces the following
-- process statement:
    -- process
    -- begin
    --    wait until DCK = '1';
    --    NREQ <= REQ;
    -- end process;
process (NREQ, DYP, DLY)
begin
    if NREQ = '1' then
        FOP <= DYP;
    else
        FOP <= DLY;
    end if;
end process;
```

The synthesized netlist for this example is shown in Figure 3-45.

3.22 Generics

Generics provide a powerful mechanism in VHDL to model parameterized designs. Here is a simple example of an N-input and gate.

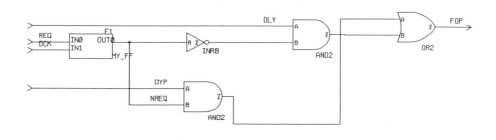

Figure 3-45 Instantiating a predefined flip-flop.

```
library IEEE;
use IEEE.STD_LOGIC_1164.all;
entity GENERIC_AND is
   generic (SIZE: INTEGER);
   port (A: STD_LOGIC_VECTOR (0 to SIZE-1);
         Z: out STD_LOGIC);
end GENERIC_AND;

architecture EXAMPLE of GENERIC_AND is
begin
   process (A)
      variable RES: STD_LOGIC;
   begin
      RES := '1';

      for K in A'RANGE loop
         RES := RES and A(K);
      end loop;

      Z <= RES;
   end process;
end EXAMPLE;
```

The entity GENERIC_AND cannot be synthesized by itself since the value
of SIZE is not yet specified. Such an entity is synthesized when it is instantiated within other entities. An example is shown next.

```
library IEEE;
use IEEE.STD_LOGIC_1164.all;
entity GENERIC_INSTANTIATE is
   port (TSQ: in STD_LOGIC_VECTOR (0 to 5);
         RSQ: out STD_LOGIC);
end;
```

```
architecture EXAMPLE of GENERIC_INSTANTIATE is
component GENERIC_AND
    generic (SIZE: INTEGER);
    port (A: in STD_LOGIC_VECTOR (0 to SIZE-1);
        Z: out STD_LOGIC);
end component;

signal SV1, SV2: STD_LOGIC;
begin
    G1: GENERIC_AND generic map (SIZE => 2)
                port map (A => TSQ(0 to 1), Z => SV1);
    G2: GENERIC_AND generic map (SIZE => 4)
                port map (A => TSQ(2 to 5), Z => SV2);
    RSQ <= SV1 xor SV2;
end;
```

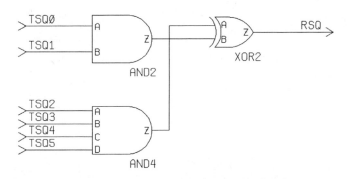

Figure 3-46 Using a 2-input and a 4-input generic and gate.

During the synthesis of entity GENERIC_INSTANTIATE , if a component instantiation with a generic map is found, the default entity is searched and the generic values are passed in before the generic entity is synthesized. In this example, the entity GENERIC_AND is synthesized twice, once for each instantiation of the generic entity. The synthesized netlist for the entity GENERIC_INSTANTIATE is shown in Figure 3-46.

3.23 Generate statement

There are two forms of the generate statement: the if-generate scheme and the for-generate scheme. A generate statement causes the concurrent statements that appear within it to be conditionally selected if it is an if-generate statement, or the concurrent statements are expanded inline if it is a for-generate statement. Here is an example of a ripple counter described using a generate statement; its synthesized netlist is shown in Figure 3-47.

```
entity RIPPLE is
    port (CLEAR, COUNT: in BIT;
          Q: out BIT_VECTOR (0 to 3));
end RIPPLE;

architecture COUNTER of RIPPLE is
    component TOGGLE_FF
        port (PC, CLK: in BIT;
              Z: out BIT);
    end component;

    signal CT: BIT_VECTOR (0 to 3);
begin
    G1: for J in 0 to 3 generate
        G2: if J = 0 generate
            T1: TOGGLE_FF port map (CLEAR, COUNT, CT(J));
        end generate G2;

        G3: if J > 0 generate
            T2: TOGGLE_FF port map (CLEAR, CT(J–1), CT(J));
        end generate G3;

        Q(J) <= CT(J);
    end generate G1;
end COUNTER;
```

Chapter 6 shows many more modeling examples that show the collective usage of many VHDL constructs.

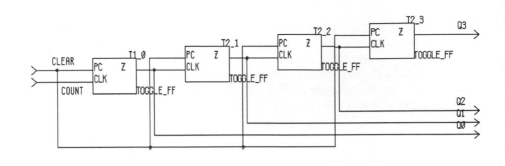

Figure 3-47 Logic generated using a generate statement.

❑

Chapter 4

Model Optimizations

This chapter describes optimizations that can be performed on a VHDL model to improve the circuit performance. In a C programming language compiler, an optimizer produces optimized machine code: code is rearranged, moved around, and so on, to reduce the C code execution time. Such optimizations may also be performed by a logic optimizer. Also in synthesis, the logic generated is very sensitive to the way a model is described. Moving a statement from one place to another or splitting up expressions may have a profound impact on the generated logic; it might increase or decrease the number of synthesized gates.

Figure 4-1 shows that different endpoints for best area and best speed are reached by a logic optimizer depending on the starting point provided by a netlist synthesized from VHDL. The various starting points are provided by rewriting the same VHDL model using different constructs. Unfortunately, no algorithms are known that determine what coding style or optimizations produce the desired balance between area and delay.

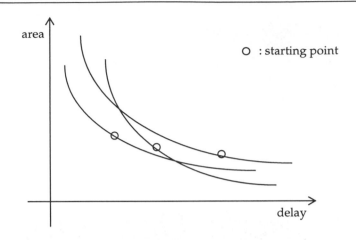

Figure 4-1 Different writing styles produce different area-delay trade-offs.

This chapter explores some of these optimizations that may be performed by a designer by rewriting appropriate code in the VHDL synthesis model. These optimizations provide a way to reduce the number of arithmetic and relational operators in the design. The overall description is more readable and easier to understand, and yields better quality designs. Synthesis and simulation times are also reduced.

4.1   Resource allocation

Resource allocation refers to the process of sharing an arithmetic-logic-unit (ALU) under mutually-exclusive conditions. Consider the following if statement.

```
if MAX > 100 then
   JAM := SAM + BAM;
else
   JAM := SAM – CAM;
end if;
```

If no resource allocation is performed, the "+" and "–" operators get synthesized into two separate ALUs. However, if resource allocation is performed, only one ALU is necessary that performs both the "+" and "–" operations. This is because the two operators are used under mutually-exclusive conditions. A multiplexer is also generated; it is needed at the second port of the multiplexer to direct inputs BAM and CAM. Figure 4-2 shows the hardware synthesized for the if statement when no resource allocation is performed. Figure 4-3 shows the same example when resource allocation is performed.

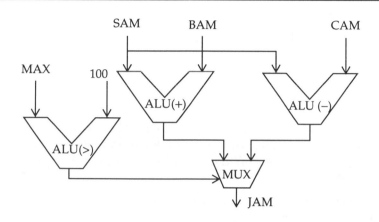

Figure 4-2 Without resource allocation.

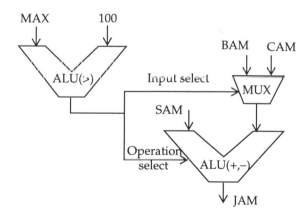

Figure 4-3 With resource allocation.

Notice that with sharing an ALU, a multiplexer has been introduced at one of the inputs of the ALU that contributes to the path delay. However, the amount of logic generated has been reduced due to sharing. This is again a trade-off that a designer has to make. In timing-critical designs, it may be better if no resource sharing is performed.

There are other variations of sharing that a synthesis tool may automatically enforce. Operators that are usually shared are:

 i. relational operators

 ii. addition

 iii. subtraction

 iv. multiplication

 v. division

Usually it is not worthwhile to generate an ALU that does an addition and a multiplication. Multiplication and division operators are typically shared amongst themselves. When sharing with other operators, the following possibilities exist:

a. Same operator, same operands: definitely must share. Example: A + B, A + B

b. Same operator, one different operand: trade-off, since one multiplexer will be introduced. Example: A + B, A + C

c. Same operator, different operands: trade-off since two multiplexers are introduced. Example: A + B, C + D

d. Different operators, same operand: useful to share. Example: A + B, A – B

e. Different operators, one different operand: trade-off since one multiplexer introduced. Example: A + B, A – C

f. Different operators, different operands: trade-off since two multiplexers introduced. Example: A + B, C – D

Possibility **a** is the best case to share followed by **d**, (**b**, **e**) and (**c**, **f**).

Resource allocation may also be performed manually by rewriting the model. Here is such an example.

```
if SHREG = '0' then
    DATAOUT := ADL + CSN;
elsif RDN = '1' then
    DATAOUT := RDN + WRN;
else
    DATAOUT := ADL + RDN;
end if;
```

```
-- After manual resource allocation:
if SHREG = '0' then
    ARG1 := ADL;
    ARG2 := CSN;
elsif RDN = '1' then
    ARG1 := RDN;
    ARG2 := WRN;
else
    ARG1 := ADL;
    ARG2 := RDN;
end if;

DATAOUT := ARG1 + ARG2;
```

The modified model uses only one adder and the multiplexers at the input ports of the adder are implied by the if statement. The original example may synthesize with three adders.

4.2   Conversion functions

VHDL is a strongly-typed language. Consequently, it is important to keep track of types in expressions and assignments. Conversion functions are often used to convert values from one type to another to maintain type compatibility. Here is an example.

```
function "+" (L, R: BIT_VECTOR) return BIT_VECTOR;

function TO_BITVECTOR (ARG, LEN: INTEGER) return BIT_VECTOR;
. . .
signal ZUT, TAR: BIT_VECTOR (3 downto 0);
. . .
ZUT <= TAR + TO_BITVECTOR (2, TAR'LENGTH);
```

Notice that it is not possible to simply write "TAR + 2" since the "+" operator is overloaded on both its operands to be of type BIT_VECTOR. Therefore to be type compatible, the conversion function TO_BITVECTOR is used.

The type conversion function really does not represent any hardware from a synthesis viewpoint, since the designer's intention is simply to add the number 2 to TAR. The conversion function is introduced as a consequence of VHDL typing rules.

Here is another example of a conversion function usage.

> **function** TO_BIT (ARG: BOOLEAN) **return** BIT;
>
> **variable** ZAB: BIT;
> . . .
> ZAB := TO_BIT (CAR > BAR);

The result of a relational operator is always of type BOOLEAN. However, per VHDL rules, it is illegal to assign a boolean value to a variable of type BIT. Therefore, a conversion function is necessary. Again, in terms of hardware, it really does not represent extra logic since the logic clearly implies to connect the output of the comparator to ZAB.

Since conversion functions do not represent hardware, it is important to find out the built-in conversion functions provided by a synthesis tool and use only these where necessary. In such cases, no extra logic is synthesized for the conversion functions.

4.3   Type INTEGER

The VHDL predefined type INTEGER represents a minimum of 32 bits in hardware (since the minimum defined range of type INTEGER is $-(2^{31}-1)$ to $+(2^{31}-1)$). In many modeling situations, it is not necessary to model an integer as 32 bits. Here is an example of such an usage.

> **variable** TIN: INTEGER;
> . . .
> TIN := TO_INTEGER (R_BUS(0 **to** 7));
> NIB := TIN + 16;

Variable TIN is declared to be of type INTEGER. However, the only assignment to it is that of an 8-bit bus. Therefore, it would be helpful (to the synthesis tool) to limit the range of the integer also to a 8-bit range with a declaration such as:

> **variable** TIN: INTEGER **range** 0 **to** 255;

A synthesis tool may generate 32 bits for TIN and realize that only the first 8 bits are used and then discard the rest. However, this is extra work for the synthesis tool to perform. Not only that, by specifying the integer constraint explicitly, a VHDL simulator can make sure that the integer value never exceeds the range.

Now consider the second assignment statement. A synthesis tool might generate a 32-bit adder first (since variable TIN is of size 32) and later realize that this was not necessary since the higher level bits were not used. Again by specifying a constraint with the type INTEGER for variable TIN, we are saving precious synthesis time, and in addition, we are placing additional constraints that can be checked for violations during a simulation.

The recommendation therefore is to use the unbounded type INTEGER only where necessary. In most of the cases, it would be better to specify a range constraint with the type INTEGER.

4.4   Common subexpressions

It is very useful in practice to identify common subexpressions and to reuse computed values where possible. Here is a simple example.

```
variable RUN: . . .
. . .
RUN := R1 + R2;
. . .
CAR :- R3 - (R1 + R2);
     Assume that the second assignment is executed every time the first
-- statement is executed. Note that this assumption may not be true if
-- either of the statements is within an if or a case statement.
```

If a synthesis tool does not identify common subexpressions, two adders would be generated, each computing the same result, that of R1 + R2. A logic optimization tool may or may not be able to identify such common logic, thus leading to larger designs. Therefore it is useful to identify common subexpressions and to reuse the computed values. For the previous example, we could replace the second assignment by:

```
CAR := R3 - RUN;
```

If the first assignment were a signal assignment (RUN would then have to be declared as a signal), such as:

signal RUN: . . .
. . .
RUN <= R1 + R3;

then a temporary variable will have to be introduced such as:

TEMP := R1 + R2;
RUN <= TEMP;
. . .
CAR := R3 – TEMP;

The problem of identifying common subexpressions becomes more important if larger blocks such as multipliers are used.

4.5   Moving code

It may so happen that within a loop statement, there is an expression whose value does not change through every iteration of the loop. Also typically a synthesis tool handles a for-loop by unrolling the loop the specified number of times. In such a case, redundant code is introduced for the expression whose value is invariant of the loop index. Again a logic optimizer may or may not be smart enough to optimize such logic. Performing the optimizations at a higher level, that is, within the model, would help the optimizer in working on more critical pieces of the code. Here is an example of such a for-loop.

CAR := . . .
. . .
for COUNT **in** 1 **to** 5 **loop**

   . . .
   TIP := CAR – 6;
   -- Assumption: CAR is not assigned a new value within the loop.

   . . .
end loop;

The right-hand-side expression in the assignment statement value is invariant of the loop index, that is, the value computed in variable TIP is independent of the loop index. However, a synthesis tool may generate five subtracters, one for each loop iteration, thus generating extra logic. In this case, only one subtracter is really necessary.

The best way to handle this case is to move the loop-invariant expression out of the loop. This also improves simulation efficiency. This is shown in the following example.

```
CAR := ...
. . .
TEMP:= CAR − 6;        -- A temporary variable is introduced.

for COUNT in 1 to 5 loop

   . . .
   TIP := TEMP;
   -- Assumption: CAR is not assigned a new value within the loop.

   . . .
end loop;
```

Such movement of code may have to be performed by the designer to produce more efficient code.

4.6   Common factoring

Common factoring is the extraction of common subexpressions in mutually-exclusive branches of an if or a case statement. Here is an example.

```
if TEST then
   AX := A and (B + C);
else
   BY := (B + C) or T;
end if;
```

The expression "B+C" is computed in mutually-exclusive branches of an if statement. However, instead of the synthesis tool generating two adders, it is useful to factor out the expression and place it before the if statement. This is shown next.

```
TEMP := B + C;          -- A temporary variable is introduced.

if TEST then
   AX := A and TEMP;
else
   BY := TEMP or T;
end if;
```

By performing this common factoring, less logic is synthesized (in the above example, only one adder gets synthesized) so that a logic optimizer may concentrate on optimizing more critical areas.

4.7   Commutativity and associativity

In certain cases, it might be necessary to perform commutative operations before performing some of the earlier mentioned optimizations. Here is an example where performing a commutative operation before common subexpression identification helps in identifying common subexpressions.

> RUN := R1 + R2;
> . . .
> CAR := R3 − (R2 + R1);

Applying commutativity rules to the expression "R2 + R1" helps in identifying the common subexpression "R1 + R2" that is also used in the first assignment.

   Similarly, associativity rules can be applied before using any of the earlier described optimizations. Here is an example.

> LAM := A + B + C;
> . . .
> BAM := C + A − B;

Notice that applying associativity and commutativity rules on the expression in the first statement identifies "C + A" as a common subexpression. After subexpression identification, the example appears like this.

> TEMP := C + A;   -- A temporary variable is introduced.
> LAM := TEMP + B;
> BAM := TEMP − B;

   If associativity and commutativity are not used, a synthesis tool may generate three adders and one subtracter; after subexpression identification, it may generate only two adders and one subtracter, thus providing increased savings in logic.

4.8   Other optimizations

There are two other optimizations that usually a synthesis tool would have no problem handling. These are

  i.   Dead-code elimination

  ii.   Constant folding

These optimizations are indeed done by the ArchSyn synthesis system and a designer usually does not have to worry about it. These optimizations are nonetheless explained below.

Dead code elimination deletes code that never gets executed. For example,

```
if 2 > 4 then
    OLI := SDY and RDY;
end if;
```

Clearly, there is no need to synthesize an and gate since the assignment statement will never get executed and represents dead code.

Constant folding implies to compute constant expressions during compile time as opposed to implementing logic and then letting a logic optimizer try getting rid of the logic. Here is a simple example.

```
constant FAC: INTEGER := 4;
. . .
YAK := 2 ** FAC;
```

Constant folding computes the value of the right-hand-side expression during compile time and assigns the value to YAK. No hardware need be generated. This leads to savings in logic optimization time.

4.9   Flip-flop and latch optimizations

4.9.1   Avoiding flip-flops

It is important to understand the flip-flop inference rules of a synthesis tool. These rules may vary from one synthesis tool to another. If the inference rules are not followed, a synthesized netlist may have many more flip-flops than are really necessary. Here is a case in point.

```
signal PS: INTEGER range 0 to 1;
signal ZOUT: BIT_VECTOR(0 to 3);
signal CLK: BIT;
. . .
process
begin
  wait until CLK = '1';

  case PS is
    when 0 =>
      PS <= 1;
      ZOUT <= "0100";
    when 1 =>
      PS <= 0;
      ZOUT <= "0001";
  end case;
end process;
```

Here the intention appears to be to store the value of signal PS in a flip-flop (rising-edge triggered). After synthesis, not only is there a flip-flop for PS, there are also four flip-flops for the signal ZOUT. This is because ZOUT is also a signal and it is being assigned under the control of a clock. It may or may not be the intention to generate flip-flops for the signal ZOUT. If not, then a case statement needs to be written in a separate process in which the signal ZOUT is assigned, this time not under the control of the clock. The modified example that generates only one flip-flop is shown next.

```
process
begin
  wait until CLK = '1';

  case PS is
    when 0 =>
      PS <= 1;
    when 1 =>
```

```
        PS <= 0;
    end case;
end process;

process (PS)
begin
    case PS is
        when 0 =>
            ZOUT <= "0100";
        when 1 =>
            ZOUT <= "0001";
    end case;
end process;
```

4.9.2   Avoiding latches

A variable or a signal that does not have a value specified in all branches of a case or an if statement can lead to a latch being built. This is because in VHDL, a variable (defined within a process) or a signal infer memory, and thus if a variable or a signal is not assigned a value in all branches of a condition, the value needs to be saved in memory. Here is an example.

```
process (PROBE, CNT)
begin
    if PROBE = '1' then
        LUCK := CNT;
    end if;
    . . .
end process;
```

What is the value of LUCK when PROBE is '0'? It must be the old value of LUCK. Thus the value of LUCK needs to be saved; a latch is created for this variable.

The best way to avoid latches is to first determine from the synthesis tool how many latches have been inferred. A designer now needs to go back and check if each latch inferred really needs to be a latch. In many cases, a designer never intended for a latch or the designer forgot to specify values under all conditions. The best rule is to check the latches that get synthesized and go back and determine why each latch got synthesized and fix code if necessary to avoid latches.

4.10 Design size

Small designs synthesize faster

Experimental studies have shown that logic circuits of size between 2000 to 5000 gates are best handled by a logic optimizer. This implies that in the VHDL model, process statements must not be inordinately long. Design should be structured into multiple processes or multiple entities.

Unfortunately, to date no correlation has been found between the gates produced and the number of lines of VHDL code. A 2500-gate circuit could have been synthesized from a 10-line VHDL code (may have a for-loop) or by 10,000 lines of VHDL code (maybe from a large case statement with simple assignments).

Synthesis run-times, mainly logic optimization, are exponential with design size. Thus it is critical to keep the sizes of subblocks within a design small.

Hierarchy

It is useful to retain the hierarchy of a VHDL model in terms of processes and blocks. This enables a hierarchy of subcircuits to be produced by the synthesis tool that a logic optimizer can effectively handle.

Quite often, a synthesis tool might automatically preserve the hierarchy of a large datapath operator. For example,

```
. . .
ZIM := RIM + SIM;          -- RIM and SIM are 16-bits.
. . .
```

In this case, a synthesis tool may preserve the 16-bit adder as a separate hierarchy. This capability is provided by the ArchSyn synthesis system.

Macros as structure

Synthesis is not the right mechanism to build a memory such as a ROM or a RAM. RAMs are usually available predefined in a technology library. When a component such as a RAM is required, it is better to treat this as a component, instantiate this in the model, and then synthesize. A synthesis tool merely creates a black box for the RAM into which the designer would later link in the RAM component.

Similar actions may be necessary if a designer has a statement of the form:

CRY := BRY * TRY;   -- 16-bit arguments.

and expects the synthesis tool to implement an efficient multiplier. The designer may have a better designed multiplier. Again in this case, it is better for the designer to instantiate a multiplier as a component, rather than expressing the multiplication operator which, upon synthesis, may or may not produce an efficient multiplier.

4.11 Using parenthesis

When writing VHDL code, the designer must be aware of the logic structure being generated. One such important point is the use of parenthesis. Here is an example.

RESULT <= RHI + RLO – PHY_DATA + MAC_RESET;

A synthesis tool when synthesizing the right-hand side-expression follows the VHDL rules for expression evaluation, that is, left to right, and builds a circuit as shown in Figure 4-4. The logic structure generated may end

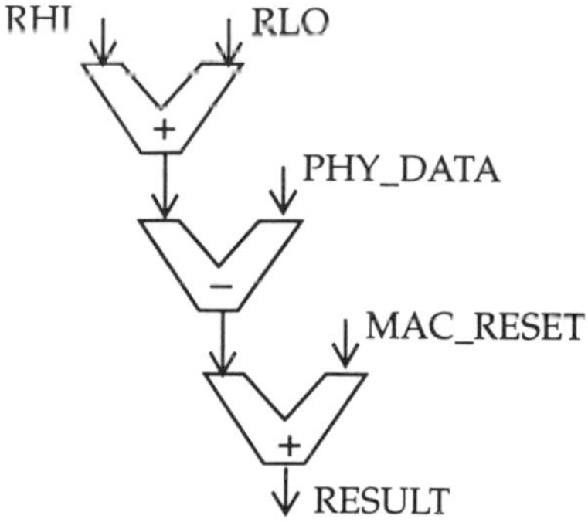

Figure 4-4 Without using parenthesis.

up having a longer critical path. A better alternative is to use parenthesis, such as

RESULT <= (RHI + RLO) – (PHY_DATA – MAC_RESET);

which results in a smaller critical path. The synthesized circuit is shown in Figure 4-5. Using parenthesis may also help identify opportunities for

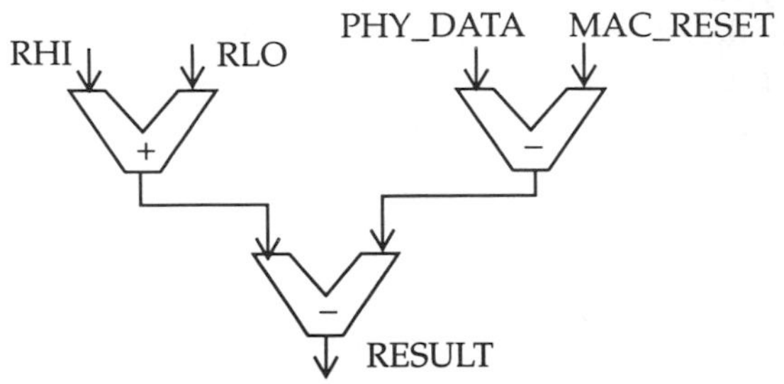

Figure 4-5 After using parenthesis.

identifying common subexpressions.

Recomendation: Use parenthesis liberally in an expression to control the structure of the synthesized logic.

4.12 Building with predefined blocks

A typical synthesis system provides a number of built-in building blocks, for example, a "+" generates an adder, and a construct such as "K := A(M)" generates a multiplexer. Sometimes a block is required that is slightly different from the one provided by the system. An example of this is that of building a 4-bit adder with both carry-in and carry-out. Here is a VHDL model that can be used to build the required adder using the built-in "+" adder. The advantage of such modeling is that other optimizations can be applied on the predefined blocks, such as resource allocation.

```
library IEEE, SYNTH;
use IEEE.STD_LOGIC_1164.all, SYNTH.STD_LOGIC_ARITH.all;
package EXTENDED is
   procedure ADD_CARRY_IO (A, B: in UNSIGNED;
                           CIN: in STD_ULOGIC;
                           signal SUM: out UNSIGNED;
                           signal COUT: out STD_ULOGIC);
```

```
      end EXTENDED;

package body EXTENDED is
  procedure ADD_CARRY_IO (A, B: in UNSIGNED;
                          CIN: in STD_ULOGIC;
                          signal SUM: out UNSIGNED;
                          signal COUT: out STD_ULOGIC) is
    variable A_TMP, B_TMP, SUM_TMP:
      UNSIGNED (A'LENGTH−1 downto 0);
  begin
    assert A'LENGTH = B'LENGTH
      report "ADD_CARRY_IO: Operand sizes do not match."
      severity ERROR;

    A_TMP := '0' & A & CIN;
    B_TMP := '0' & B & '1';
    SUM_TMP := A_TMP + B_TMP;
    SUM <= SUM_TMP (A'LENGTH−1 downto 0);
    COUT <= SUM_TMP (A'LENGTH);
  end ADD_CARRY_IO;
end;

library IEEE, SYNTH;
use IEEE.STD_LOGIC_1164.all, SYNTH.STD_LOGIC_ARITH.all;
use WORK.EXTENDED.all;
entity BIG_BLOCK is
  port (ZA, ZB: in UNSIGNED (0 to 3);
        ZCIN: in STD_ULOGIC;
        ZSUM: out UNSIGNED (0 to 3);
        ZCOUT: out STD_ULOGIC);
end;

architecture PROC_CALL of BIG_BLOCK is
begin
  ADD_CARRY_IO (A => ZA, B => ZB, CIN => ZCIN,
          SUM => ZSUM, COUT => ZCOUT);
end PROC_CALL;
```

❑

Chapter 5

Verification

Having synthesized a VHDL behavioral model into a netlist, it is important to verify the functionality of the synthesized netlist to ensure it still matches the intended functionality. This step is important since a synthesis tool may make certain assumptions or interpretations of the VHDL code that may not match those intended by the model writer.

In this chapter, we assume that this verification step is performed using simulation which verifies the functionality between the behavioral model and the synthesized netlist. We illustrate some cases of simulation mismatches that might possibly occur, describe their cause, and provide recommendations on avoiding these.

5.1   Entity interface

In this chapter, we assume that the synthesis process produces a synthesized netlist in VHDL as shown in Figure 5-1. A VHDL netlist is a collection of component instances interconnected by signals. When describing a
netlist in VHDL, it is necessary to associate type information with each
signal as well. For example, should the type of the signal be? BIT,
STD_ULOGIC, STD_LOGIC or MVL7? This is a design modeling choice;
that is, it depends on how many values are to be used in simulation to
model a signal. In this chapter, we assume that type STD_ULOGIC is
used as a basic type for all signals in a netlist.

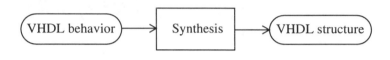

Figure 5-1 A netlist is produced from synthesis.

Having selected a type for modeling a signal in a netlist, there might
be a potential conflict with the behavioral entity if it uses different types.
Here is an example of such an entity declaration.

```
library ATTLIB;
use ATTLIB.MVL_PACKAGE.all;
entity DIV is
    port (CK, RESET, TESTN : in MVL;
          ENA : out MVL);
end DIV;

library IEEE;
use IEEE.STD_LOGIC_1164.all;
entity DIV_STR is
    port (CK, RESET, TESTN: in STD_ULOGIC;
          ENA: out STD_ULOGIC);
end DIV_STR;
```

Since the stimulus was originally defined for the behavioral entity (it generates MVL values), the stimulus file also has to be suitably modified so
that it can be applied to the structural entity. We shall later see that writ-

ing a VHDL test bench for verification eases this problem a little since conversion functions can be used in the test bench.

Similar problems occur if the behavioral entity has ports of any type other than the STD_ULOGIC, for example, a record type, integer type, or a boolean type.

5.2   *A test bench*

One approach to verifying functionality is to simulate the VHDL structural model with the same set of stimulus as used during behavioral simulation, save the results in a results file and compare to see if the results are identical. The stimulus file may have to be modified if a port type in the behavioral model is any other than type STD_ULOGIC. This scenario is shown in Figure 5-2.

Another approach is to write a test bench; a test bench is a model written in VHDL that applies stimulus, compares the output responses, and reports any simulation mismatches. Conversion functions are used within the test bench to convert stimulus values to type STD_ULOGIC. Figure 5-3 shows such a scenario. A test bench for a model called DIV is shown next. The stimulus is read from a vector file "INPUTS.VEC"; its contents are of the form:

```
T'100
T'000
T'101
. . .

library IEEE, SYNTH;
use IEEE.STD_LOGIC_1164.all, SYNTH.STD_LOGIC_ARITH.all;
use STD.TEXTIO.all;
entity DIV_TB is end;

use WORK.TSG_VHDL.all;
architecture TEST_BENCH of DIV_TB is
   -- Component declarations:
   component DIV port (
      CK: in STD_ULOGIC;
      RESET: in STD_ULOGIC;
      TESTN: in STD_ULOGIC;
      ENA: out STD_ULOGIC
   ); end component;      -- The behavioral component.
```

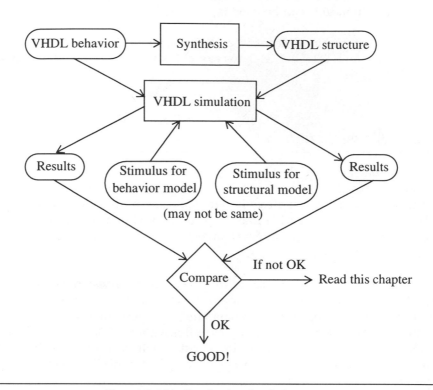

Figure 5-2 Verification by simulation.

```
component DIV_STR port (
  CK: in STD_ULOGIC;
  RESET: in STD_ULOGIC;
  TESTN: in STD_ULOGIC;
  ENA: out STD_ULOGIC
); end component;              -- The structural component.

-- Configuration specifications:
for all: DIV use entity WORK.DIV;
for all: DIV_STR use configuration WORK.DIV_STR_STR_CON;

-- Input and output signals:
signal CK_BEH_IN: STD_ULOGIC;
signal RESET_BEH_IN: STD_ULOGIC;
signal TESTN_BEH_IN: STD_ULOGIC;
signal ENA_BEH_OUT: STD_ULOGIC;
signal CK_STR_IN: STD_ULOGIC;
```

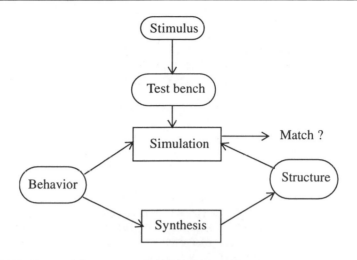

Figure 5-3 Using a common test bench.

```
signal RESET_STR_IN: STD_ULOGIC;
signal TESTN_STR_IN: STD_ULOGIC;
signal ENA_STR_OUT: STD_ULOGIC;
begin
  -- Component instantiations:
  BEH: DIV port map (CK_BEH_IN, RESET_BEH_IN,
            TESTN_BEH_IN, ENA_BEH_OUT);
  STR: DIV_STR port map (CK_STR_IN, RESET_STR_IN,
            TESTN_STR_IN, ENA_STR_OUT);

  -- Read vector file and compare:
  process
    file VEC_FILE: TEXT is in "INPUTS.VEC";
    variable IN_BUF, OUT_BUF: LINE;
    variable TOT_VECTORS: NATURAL;
  begin
    while not ENDFILE (VEC_FILE) loop
      IN_BUF := null;
      READLINE (VEC_FILE, IN_BUF);

      -- Skip iteration if not a Tquote vector in file:
      if IN_BUF(1) /= 'T' then
        next;
      end if;

      TOT_VECTORS := TOT_VECTORS + 1;
      -- Get vector starting from index 3:
```

```
                    CK_BEH_IN <= TO_STDULOGIC (IN_BUF(3));
                    RESET_BEH_IN <= TO_STDULOGIC (IN_BUF(4));
                    TESTN_BEH_IN <= TO_STDULOGIC (IN_BUF(5));
                    CK_STR_IN <= TO_STDULOGIC (IN_BUF(3));
                    RESET_STR_IN <= TO_STDULOGIC (IN_BUF(4));
                    TESTN_STR_IN <= TO_STDULOGIC (IN_BUF(5));

                    wait for 1 ns; -- Wait for logic to settle.

                    -- Compare outputs:
                    if
                       NOT_EQUALS(ENA_BEH_OUT, ENA_STR_OUT)
                    then
                       WRITE (OUT_BUF, STRING'("**** MISMATCH " &
                         "ERROR: Outputs do not match on vector "));
                       WRITE (OUT_BUF, TOT_VECTORS);
                       WRITE (OUT_BUF, STRING'(" at time "));
                       WRITE (OUT_BUF, NOW);
                       WRITE (OUT_BUF, STRING'(":  ("));
                       WRITE (OUT_BUF, TO_CHARACTER (ENA_BEH_OUT));
                       WRITE (OUT_BUF, STRING'(" <---> "));
                       WRITE (OUT_BUF, TO_CHARACTER (ENA_STR_OUT));
                       WRITE (OUT_BUF, STRING'(")"));
                       WRITELINE (OUTPUT, OUT_BUF);
                    end if;
                 end loop;

                 report "Completed running testbench"
                    severity NOTE;

                 wait;                  -- Done verification.
              end process;
           end;
```

Note the use of conversion functions to convert stimulus values to type
STD_ULOGIC and also their use in converting the observed results of the
behavioral model into type STD_ULOGIC so that a comparison can be
made. The function NOT_EQUALS returns false if the two operands are
the same or if either is an 'X' or an 'U'. This test bench model prints all
mismatch violations that occurs.

   In the following sections, we see examples of how mismatches may
occur.

5.3   Delays in assignment statements

Delays specified in a behavioral model may potentially cause a mismatch in simulation results. Here is an example of a behavioral model and its synthesized netlist.

```
library SYNTH;
use SYNTH.STD_LOGIC_ARITH.all;
entity ADDER is
    port (A, B: in UNSIGNED(0 to 3);
          C: out UNSIGNED (0 to 3));
end;

architecture TEST of ADDER is
begin
    C <= A + B after 5 ns;
end TEST;

-- The synthesized netlist is:
library IEEE;
use IEEE.STD_LOGIC_1164.all;
entity ADDER is
    port (A0, A1, A2, A3, B0, B1, B2, B3: in STD_ULOGIC;
          C0, C1, C2, C3: out STD_ULOGIC);
end ADDER;

architecture ADDER_STR of ADDER is
    signal C2_1, S248, S310, S241, S244, S295, S299, S242, S243, S291,
          S237, S238, S239, S240, S334, S235, S236: STD_ULOGIC;
begin
    C0_1: OAI21 port map (C2_1, S248, S310, C0);
    S310_1: ND2 port map (S248, C2_1, S310);
    S248_1: XOR2 port map (A0, B0, S248);
    C2_2: AOI22 port map (S241, S244, A1, B1, C2_1);
    C1_1: OAI22 port map (S295, S244, S299, S241, C1);
    S299_1: INRB port map (S244, S299);
    S244_1: OAI22 port map (B1, S242, A1, S243, S244);
    S243_1: INRB port map (B1, S243);
    S242_1: INRB port map (A1, S242);
    S295_1: INRB port map (S241, S295);
    S241_1: OAI22 port map (S291, S237, S238, S239, S241);
    S291_1: INRB port map (S240, S291);
    C2_1: OAI21 port map (S237, S240, S334, C2);
    S334_1: ND2 port map (S237, S240, S334);
    S240_1: OAI22 port map (B2, S238, A2, S239, S240);
    S239_1: INRB port map (B2, S239);
```

```
         S238_1: INRB port map (A2, S238);
         S237_1: ND2 port map (A3, B3, S237);
         C3_1: OAI22 port map (B3, S235, A3, S236, C3);
         S236_1: INRB port map (B3, S236);
         S235_1: INRB port map (A3, S235);
      end ADDER_STR;
```

If the vectors from a stimulus file were applied, say every 1 ns, and all the components in the netlist represent behavioral models with no delay, the results from the behavior and structure model will be skewed. The correct approach in such a case is:

i.   either to delete all delays from the behavioral model (which may be too much to ask for!)

ii. or to apply the stimulus with a period greater than 5ns: a much better rule.

Thus to avoid delays in a behavioral model from causing simulation mismatches, the maximum delay in a behavioral model must be computed. The stimulus application time must be greater than this maximum delay.

When delays are present in the models for the library components, these delays must also be considered in determining the stimulus period.

5.4   Unconnected ports

It could happen that a structural model has a component with an unconnected input port. Such a case is shown in the following example.

```
entity AOI22 is
   port (A, B, D: in BIT;
         Z: out BIT);
end AOI22;

architecture TEST of AOI22 is
begin
   process (A, B, D)
      variable T1, T2, C: BIT;
   begin
      T1 := A and B
      T2 := C and D;              -- Note that C is not assigned anywhere.
      Z <= not (T1 or T2);
   end process;
```

```
end;

-- Its synthesized netlist is:
library IEEE;
use IEEE.STD_LOGIC_1164.all;
entity AOI22_STR is
   port (A, B, D: in STD_ULOGIC;
        Z: out STD_ULOGIC);
end AOI22_STR;

architecture AOI22_STR of AOI22_STR is
   component AND2
      port (INPUT_1, INPUT_2: in STD_ULOGIC;
           OUTPUT_1: out STD_ULOGIC);
   end component;

   component INRB
      port (INPUT_1: in STD_ULOGIC;
           OUTPUT_1: out STD_ULOGIC);
   end component;

   component OR2
      port (INPUT_1, INPUT_2: in STD_ULOGIC;
           OUTPUT_1: out STD_ULOGIC);
   end component;

   signal T1_1, T2_1, T2_0 : STD_ULOGIC;
begin
   S0_1: AND2 port map (INPUT_1=>A, INPUT_2=>B,
              OUTPUT_1=> T1_1);
   S1_1: AND2 port map (INPUT_1=>open, INPUT_2=>D,
              OUTPUT_1=> T2_1);
   S2_1: OR2 port map (INPUT_1=>T1_1, INPUT_2=> T2_1,
              OUTPUT_1=>T2_0);
   S3_1: INRB port map (INPUT_1=>T2_0, OUTPUT_1=>Z);
end AOI22_STR;
   -- Note: A logic optimizer has not yet been used; it could
   -- potentially remove such a gate.
```

In order for the entity AOI22_STR to compile, a default value must be specified for the first port of component AND2. Question is, what must be its value? '0', '1', or 'U'? During behavioral simulation, the value of C used is a '0'; this is the leftmost value of type BIT. Therefore in structural simulation as well, the default value of the port for component AND2 must be set to '0', otherwise a simulation mismatch may occur.

Recommendation: A good synthesis tool such as the ArchSyn synthesis system will issue warning messages about a value used before being defined (such as variable C in the above example). Heed these warnings.

5.5   *Signals vs. variables*

If a signal is used instead of a variable to hold a temporary value in a set of sequential statements, simulation mismatches can occur as shown in the following example.

```
process (CCK)
begin
  if CCK'EVENT and CCK = '1' then
    SPI_PLD <= PI_PLD;
  end if;

  ICA_SRN <= SPI_PLD;
end process;
```

SPI_PLD is a signal that is assigned a value in an if statement and its value is later assigned to signal ICA_SRN. Mismatches will potentially occur since changes to SPI_PLD do not propagate to ICA_SRN at the same time. This behavior does not occur in the corresponding structural model; the output of the flip-flop SPI_PLD is connected directly to signal ICA_SRN.

Here the correct intention was to use SPI_PLD as a temporary and thus to be make it a variable. Alternately, the signal assignment could be moved out of the process, or signal SPI_PLD could be put on the sensitivity list of the process.

Here is another example.

```
process (RESET, CCK, ZT)
begin
  if CCK'EVENT and CCK='1' then
    DZ(0) <= ZT;

    for J in 0 to 2 loop
      DZ(J+1) <= DZ(J);
    end loop;
```

```
      Z1 <= DZ(3);
   end if;

      ZOUT <= Z1;
   end process;
```

There are three dangerous conflicts here. Signal DZ(0) (also DZ(1) and DZ(2)) is being assigned and then used. Signal DZ(3) is being assigned and then used. Signal Z1 is assigned and then used. DZ and Z1 should be modeled as variables if mismatches are to be avoided.

Recommendation: Check to see if there are any signals that are being assigned and then later read in the process. To prevent mismatches, it is better to model such temporaries as variables.

5.6   Inertial and transport delays

Delays are often ignored by synthesis tools, as is the case with the ArchSyn synthesis system. The fact that it is ignored may simply cause simulation results to differ between the synthesized netlist and the behavior model. A case in point.

```
      LX <= '1' after 3 ns;

   if COND then
      LX <= '0' after 5 ns;
      . . .
```

Behavioral simulation shows a value of '1' on signal LX after 3 ns and the value going to '0' after 5 ns if the condition COND is true. However, since a synthesis tool ignores delays, if COND is true, the net effect is as if '0' is assigned to LX and the appropriate hardware gets synthesized to reflect this. Notice that if the synthesized netlist is simulated, the value of signal LX will not go to '1' if COND is true.

Recommendation: Avoid inserting delays into a behavioral model that is to be synthesized. If necessary, lump total delays for a signal in one place.

5.7   Resolution function

A synthesis tool may treat a resolution function in a different way than that specified by the function itself. For example, in the ArchSyn system, any resolution function specified in a signal declaration is ignored and a global option is specified on how to treat signals that are driven by more than one source. Since the synthesis system treats the resolution function as a special case, simulation mismatches can potentially occur.

Here is an example.

> **signal** Z : WIRED_OR BIT;
>
> . . .
>
> Z <= TO_BIT (CLY);
>
> . . .
>
> Z <= LA **or** BL;

In behavioral simulation, the values of the two drivers for signal Z are passed to the WIRED_OR resolution function and its return value becomes the effective value for signal Z.

However in the ArchSyn system, assuming that an "and drivers" option is specified, the synthesized netlist will connect the drivers of signal Z using an and gate. This is shown in Figure 5-4. This functionality is different from the functionality of the behavioral model and simulation mismatches may occur.

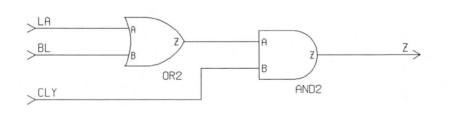

Figure 5-4 Inserting an explicit gate for modeling a resolution function.

Recommendation: Avoid having two or more drivers for a signal, thus obviating the need for a resolution function. If a resolution function is necessary, use only one type of resolution function in a behavioral model and specify the same or its equivalent as an option to the synthesis tool.

5.8   Built-in types and functions

A synthesis system typically supports two types of built-in functions:

    i.   conversion functions

    ii. arithmetic functions

Conversion functions are used to convert values from one type to another type. These functions merely transfer data from one type to another (so as to conform to VHDL's strong typing rules) and are not meant to be synthesized as hardware logic; a synthesis system often recognizes these functions as built-ins and does not generate any extra logic; that is, the conversion function body is not synthesized. Examples of conversion functions are:

> **function** TO_INTEGER (ARG: BIT_VECTOR) **return** INTEGER;
> **function** TO_STDLOGICVECTOR (ARG: INTEGER; SIZE: NATURAL)
>   **return** STD_LOGIC_VECTOR;

Arithmetic functions of certain predefined types are similarly built-in into a synthesis system. Examples are:

> **function** "+" (L, R: UNSIGNED) **return** UNSIGNED;
> **function** "– " (L: SIGNED; R: INTEGER) **return** SIGNED;

When using such built-in arithmetic functions, care must be taken in modifying the body of the arithmetic function. Otherwise, it could lead to simulation mismatches; the synthesis system may synthesize the built-in function, whereas during behavioral simulation, the function body is simulated.

Recommendation: Find out the built-in functions provided by a synthesis system and use these. Do not modify the built-in functions. If a change is necessary, create a separate package and then use the function from this package.

5.9   Sensitivity list

Quite often, a synthesis system like the ArchSyn system ignores a sensitivity list of a process during synthesis. This can lead to simulation mismatches if proper care is not taken in modeling. Here is a simple example.

```
SENSE: process (RD)
begin
   GT <= RD and CK;
end process;
```

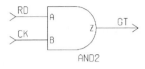

Figure 5-5 Netlist is sensitive to both signal RD and CK.

The synthesized structural model, as shown in Figure 5-5, evaluates on all changes of signals RD and CK, while the behavioral model executes only on changes to signal RD.

Here is another example of a process with an incomplete sensitivity list that causes simulation mismatches.

```
signal VAL: UNSIGNED (MAXSIZE–1 downto 0);
signal COUNTER: UNSIGNED (VAL'LEFT downto 0);

. . .
CNT_PRC: process (RESET, CCK, ENA)
begin
   COUNT (COUNTER, CCK, RESET, ENA);
   VAL <= COUNTER;
end process;
```

In this example, the signal COUNTER is not in the sensitivity list of the process and thus any changes made by procedure COUNT to signal COUNTER do not affect the value of VAL. Signal VAL gets updated with the value of COUNTER next time when there is an event on signal RESET, CCK or ENA. In this example, the signal assignment statement must be moved outside the process so that any changes of value on COUNTER gets automatically updated into VAL. Alternately, COUNTER could also have been placed in the sensitivity list of the process (this could potentially create extra simulation cycles).

Here is another example of a process with an incomplete sensitivity list that may cause simulation mismatches.

```
signal RST: BIT;
signal PBUS, TREG: STD_LOGIC_VECTOR (3 downto 0);
. . .
process (RST)
begin
  if RST = '1' then
    TREG <= (others => '0');
  else
    TREG <= PBUS;
  end if;
end process;
```

The signal PBUS is not in the sensitivity list of the process. However in
the synthesized netlist, any changes on PBUS will propagate into TREG if
the if condition is false. This is not consistent with the behavioral model
and thus a simulation mismatch occurs.

   Recommendation: For a process without a wait statement, include
all signals read in the process in the sensitivity list of the process.

5.10 Initialization

VHDL provides a convenient way to specify the initial state of a circuit (re-
minder: a state of a circuit may be modeled using a variable or a signal).
The initial state can be specified by specifying an initial value for the variable or the signal in its declaration. Unfortunately, such an initialization
is not supported by most synthesis tools, including ArchSyn, since no reset
signal is specified. A simulator has no problem in initializing the state by
using the initial value; however, in hardware, registers usually start in an
unknown state when they are powered on.

   A typical synthesis system, including the ArchSyn system, therefore
ignore initial values specified for a variable or a signal in its declaration.
This can cause a mismatch in simulation results. Here is an example that
illustrates this problem. In this example, the state of the circuit is stored
in the variable SPEED_STATE.

```
library IEEE;
use IEEE.STD_LOGIC_1164.all;
entity CAR_CTRL is
  port (ACCELERATOR, BRAKE, CLK: in STD_LOGIC;
        SPEED: out STD_LOGIC_VECTOR(1 downto 0));
```

```
   end CAR_CTRL;

architecture CAR_CTRL of CAR_CTRL is
begin
  process (ACCELERATOR, BRAKE, CLK)
    variable SPEED_STATE: STD_LOGIC_VECTOR (1 downto 0) := "10";
  begin
    if CLK = '1' and CLK'EVENT then
      if ACCELERATOR = '1' then
        case SPEED_STATE is
          when "00" =>
            SPEED_STATE := "01";
          when "01" =>
            SPEED_STATE := "10";
          when "10" =>
            SPEED_STATE := "11";
          when "11" =>
            SPEED_STATE := "11";
          when others =>
            null;
        end case;
      elsif BRAKE = '1' then
        case SPEED_STATE is
          when "00" =>
            SPEED_STATE := "00";
          when "01" =>
            SPEED_STATE := "00";
          when "10" =>
            SPEED_STATE := "01";
          when "11" =>
            SPEED_STATE := "10";
          when others =>
            null;
        end case;
      else
        null;   -- Speed does not change.
      end if;
    end if;

    SPEED <= SPEED_STATE;
  end process;
end CAR_CTRL;
```

If the synthesis system ignores the initial value of variable
SPEED_STATE, the flip-flops generated for the variable SPEED_STATE
do not get initialized to their initial value. This can be seen from the following synthesized netlist.

```
library IEEE;
use IEEE.STD_LOGIC_1164.all;
entity CAR_CTRL_STR is
   port (ACCELERATOR, BRAKE, CLK: in STD_ULOGIC;
         SPEED: out STD_ULOGIC_VECTOR(1 downto 0));
end CAR_CTRL_STR;

library SYNTH;
use SYNTH.GENERIC_COMP.all;
architecture CAR_CTRL_STR of CAR_CTRL_STR is
   signal SPEED_1: STD_ULOGIC_VECTOR(1 downto 0);
   signal DSPEED_STATE0_1, DSPEED_STATE1_1, NET0, S198, S227,
         S237, L0011_1, S201, S159: STD_ULOGIC;
begin
   S1_1: FD1S3AX port map (D=>DSPEED_STATE1_1,
             CK=>CLK, Q=>SPEED_1(1), QN=>open);
   S0_1: FD1S3AX port map (D=>DSPEED_STATE0_1,
             CK=>CLK, Q=>SPEED_1(0), QN=>NET0);
   DSPEED_STATE1_2: OAI211 port map (A1=>S198,
             A2=>NET0, B=>S227, C=>S237, Z=>DSPEED_STATE1_1);
   S237_1: OAI21 port map (A1=>SPEED_1(0),
             A2=>L0011_1, B=>SPEED_1(1), Z=>S237);
   L0011_2: NR2 port map (A=>BRAKE,
             B=>ACCELERATOR, Z=>L0011_1);
   S198_1: INRB port map (A=>ACCELERATOR, Z=>S198);
   DSPEED_STATE0_2: OAI221 port map (A1=>NET0, A2=>S201,
             B1=>SPEED_1(0), B2=>S159, C=>S227,
             Z=>DSPEED_STATE0_1);
   S227_1: ND2 port map (A=>SPEED_1(1), B=>ACCELERATOR,
             Z=>S227);
   S159_1: AOI21 port map (A1=>SPEED_1(1), A2=>BRAKE,
             B=>ACCELERATOR, Z=>S159);
   S201_1: OR2 port map (A=>BRAKE, B=>ACCELERATOR, Z=>S201);
   SPEED(1) <= SPEED_1(1);
   SPEED(0) <= SPEED_1(0);
end CAR_CTRL_STR;
```

Thus while the behavioral model starts with an initial value of "10" for SPEED_STATE, the structural model behaves differently, that is, the flip-flops get initialized to "UU", unless the synthesized netlist is manually modified by assigning an initial value for the flip-flops. This is shown in the following skeleton code of the synthesized netlist.

```
architecture CAR_CTRL_STR of CAR_CTRL_STR is
  signal SPEED_1: STD_ULOGIC_VECTOR(1 downto 0) := "10";
  signal DSPEED_STATE0_1,
  . . .
```

The recommended approach is to explicitly model the initial value as part of the behavior, as is shown in the following modified model. A new signal, RESET, needs to be introduced.

```
library IEEE;
use IEEE.STD_LOGIC_1164.all;
entity CAR_CTRL is
  port (ACCELERATOR, BRAKE, CLK, RESET: in STD_LOGIC;
       SPEED: out STD_LOGIC_VECTOR(1 downto 0));
end CAR_CTRL;

architecture CAR_CTRL of CAR_CTRL is
begin
  process (ACCELERATOR, BRAKE, CLK, RESET)
    variable SPEED_STATE: STD_LOGIC_VECTOR (1 downto 0);
  begin
    if RESET = '1' then              -- Asynchronous reset.
      SPEED_STATE := "10";
    elsif CLK = '1' and CLK'EVENT then
      if ACCELERATOR = '1' then
        case SPEED_STATE is
          when "00" =>
            SPEED_STATE := "01";
          when "01" =>
            SPEED_STATE := "10";
          when "10" =>
            SPEED_STATE := "11";
          when "11" =>
            SPEED_STATE := "11";
          when others =>
            null;
        end case;
      elsif BRAKE = '1' then
        case SPEED_STATE is
          when "00" =>
            SPEED_STATE := "00";
          when "01" =>
            SPEED_STATE := "00";
          when "10" =>
            SPEED_STATE := "01";
          when "11" =>
            SPEED_STATE := "10";
```

```
            when others =>
                null;
          end case;
       else
           null;   -- Speed does not change
          end if;
       end if;


    SPEED <= SPEED_STATE;
  end process;
end CAR_CTRL;
```

5.11 Using attribute ENUM_TYPE_ENCODING

Consider the following model that uses a signal of an enumeration type.
The encoding for the enumeration literals of the enumeration type are explicitly specified using the attribute ENUM_TYPE_ENCODING.

```
architecture ENCODING of ENGINE is
   type CAR_SPEED is (STOP, SLOW, MEDIUM, FAST);
   signal SPEED: CAR_SPEED;
   attribute ENUM_TYPE_ENCODING: BOOLEAN;
   attribute ENUM_TYPE_ENCODING of CAR_SPEED: type
           is "1000 0100 0010 0001";
begin
  process . . .
  begin
    . . .
    if SPEED > SLOW then
       BRAKE <= TRUE;
    else
       BRAKE <= FALSE;
    end if;
    . . .
  end process;
end ENCODING;
```

The attribute ENUM_TYPE_ENCODING is a special attribute recognized
only by the ArchSyn synthesis system; it is not necessarily recognized by
every simulation system. Consequently, during behavioral simulation, the
condition SPEED > SLOW will be true for SPEED values of MEDIUM or
FAST. However, in the synthesized netlist, STOP (with value "1000") is

greater than SLOW (with value "0100"), thus causing simulation mismatches.

Recommendation: When   using   attribute
ENUM_TYPE_ENCODING, avoid using relational operators <, <=, >, >=,
since the values of these depend on the encoding of the states, which may
not be understood by a simulation system.

❑

Chapter 6

Modeling Hardware Elements for Synthesis

In Chapter 3, we looked at the synthesis of VHDL into gates. In this chapter we continue to describe the synthesis process by starting with the familiar elements that a logic designer uses and show how to describe these in VHDL. Some of the examples are similar to the ones in Chapter 3, but a number of other aspects of synthesis are brought out. As before, we show both the VHDL input to synthesis and the schematic for the output circuitry.

This chapter also provides a number of VHDL synthesis examples. These models illustrate the usage of VHDL constructs collectively to model a design that can be synthesized.

6.1   Modeling a wire

A wire can be modeled using a signal. A variable can also be used to model a wire; however, multiple assignments to the same variable are considered as different instances of a wire. Consider the following model of a 2-by-1 multiplexer with an enable signal.

```
library IEEE;
use IEEE.STD_LOGIC_1164.all;
entity MUX2x1 is
    port (A, B, SEL, ENA: in STD_LOGIC;
         ZQ: out STD_LOGIC);
end MUX2x1;

architecture SIG_WIRES of MUX2x1 is
    signal TRA, TRB, TOR: STD_LOGIC;
begin
    TRA <= A and SEL;
    TRB <= B and (not SEL);
    TOR <= TRA or TRB;
    ZQ <= TOR when ENA = '1' else 'Z';
end SIG_WIRES;
```

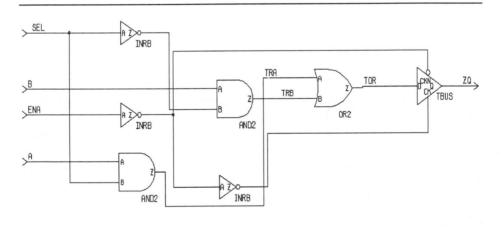

Figure 6-1 A signal becomes a wire.

In this case, signals TRA, TRB, and TOR are wires. Figure 6-1 shows the synthesized netlist. Here is the same example, but this time, variables are used.

```
architecture VAR_WIRES of MUX2x1 is
begin
  process (A, B, SEL, ENA)
    variable TA, TB: STD_LOGIC;
  begin
    TA := A and SEL;
    TB := B and (not SEL);
    TA := TA or TB;

    if ENA = '1' then
      ZQ <= TA;
    else
      ZQ <= 'Z';
    end if;
  end process;
end VAR_WIRES;
```

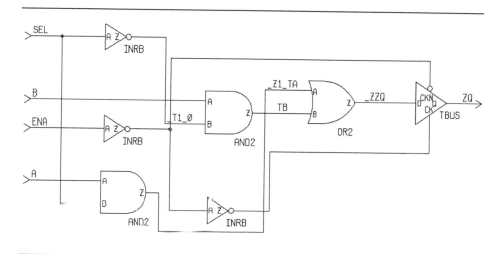

Figure 6-2 A variable is also a wire.

TA and TB are variables in the process. Variable TA is assigned twice. However the different assignments are considered as different instances of a wire. The synthesized netlist is shown in Figure 6-2.

6.2   Modeling combinational logic

The best way for describing combinational logic is to use concurrent signal assignment statements. A process statement can also be used to describe combinational logic; however, the synthesized logic may not be apparent from the description. If combinational logic is described using concurrent signal assignment statements, the synthesized logic is implicit in the description. Consider the model of a built-in self-test cell.

```
library IEEE;
use IEEE.STD_LOGIC_1164.all;
entity BIST_CELL is
    port (B0, B1, D0, D1: in STD_LOGIC;
          Z: out STD_LOGIC);
end BIST_CELL;

architecture CONC_SIG of BIST_CELL is
    signal S1, S2, S3, S4: STD_LOGIC;
begin
    S1 <= B0 nand D1;
    S2 <= D0 nand B1;
    S3 <= S2 nor S1;
    S4 <= S2 and S1;
    Z <= S4 nor S3;
end CONC_SIG;
```

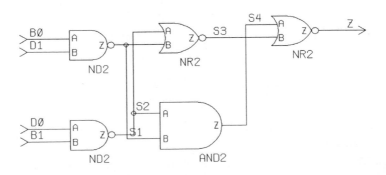

Figure 6-3 Combinational logic from concurrent signal assignments.

The synthesized circuit is shown in Figure 6-3. Notice the structure of the synthesized circuit is very similar to that of the concurrent signal assignment statements. Here is the same model, but this time the cell is described using a process statement.

```
architecture PROCESS_EX of BIST_CELL is
begin
  process (B0, D0, B1, D1)
    variable S1, S2: STD_LOGIC;
    begin
      S1 := B0 nand D1;
      S2 := D0 nand B1;
      S1 := S2 nor S1;
      S2 := S2 and S1;
      Z <= S1 nor S2;
    end process;
end PROCESS_EX;
```

Notice that variables S1 and S2 are used as temporaries in more than one place and do not represent one wire. The synthesized circuit still remains the same as that shown in Figure 6-3; however, the one-to-one mapping between the variables in the process and the nets in the synthesized structure is not present.

6.3   Modeling synchronous logic

The behavior of synchronous logic can be described by using a process statement of a special form. This is of the form:

```
process
begin          -- First statement has to be a wait statement.
  wait until clock_edge;
  -- Synchronous logic described here since all statements execute
  -- only if clock edge occurs.
end process;
```

where *clock_edge* is one of

```
clock_name = logic-0
clock_name = logic-1
RISING_EDGE (clock_name)
FALLING_EDGE (clock_name)
```

The last two forms of clock edge can only be used if the clock signal is of type STD_ULOGIC or STD_LOGIC. Here is an example of such a process.

```
library IEEE;
use IEEE.STD_LOGIC_1164.all;
entity PICK_ONE is
   port (A, B, CLK, CTRL: in STD_LOGIC;
         Z: out STD_LOGIC);
end;

architecture SYNC of PICK_ONE is
begin
   process
   begin
     wait until CLK = '0';

     if CTRL = '1' then
       Z <= A;
     else
       Z <= B;
     end if;
   end process;
end SYNC;
```

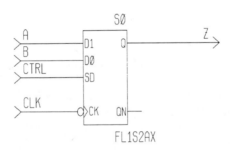

Figure 6-4 Synchronous logic synthesized using a special process statement.

The assignment to signal Z happens only at the falling edge of a clock. The synthesized circuit is shown in Figure 6-4. Signal Z is inferred to be a falling-edge-triggered flip-flop. The flip-flop shown in the figure has a data-select, that is, the signal CTRL selects either A or B as the data for the flip-flop.

6.4   Modeling a flip-flop

6.4.1   From a signal

If a signal is assigned a value under the control of a clock edge, a flip-flop is generated.

```
entity FLIP_FLOP is
   port (CLK: in BIT;
         CURRENT_STATE: in INTEGER range 0 to 15;
         NEXT_STATE: out INTEGER range 0 to 15);
end FLIP_FLOP;

architecture INFER of FLIP_FLOP is
begin
   process
   begin
     wait until CLK = '1';            -- Rising clock edge.
     NEXT_STATE <= CURRENT_STATE;
   end process;
end INFER;
```

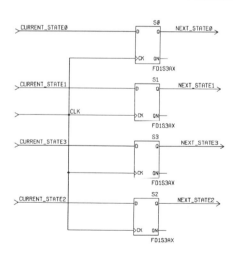

Figure 6-5 Flip-flops inferred from a signal assigned under clock control.

In this example, signal NEXT_STATE is assigned a value only if there is a rising edge on signal CLK. Thus, four rising-edge-triggered flip-flops (need to store values 0 through 15) are inferred for signal NEXT_STATE. This is shown in Figure 6-5.

If a falling-edge-triggered flip-flop needs to be inferred, then the wait statement needs to be replaced by the following wait statement.

> **wait until** CLK = '0';

6.4.2   From a variable

A variable assigned under the control of a clock may or may not be inferred a flip-flop. This depends on whether the value of the variable is defined and then used, or if it is used first and then defined. In the former case, no flip-flop need be inferred, while in the latter case, a flip-flop has to be inferred. Let us look at the case where a variable is defined before use and it is assigned a value under the control of a clock.

```
process
    variable TEMP: INTEGER range 0 to 15;
begin
    wait until CLK = '1';
    TEMP := CURRENT_STATE;
    NEXT_STATE <= TEMP;
end process;
```

No flip-flops are inferred for variable TEMP since a value is assigned to the variable and used immediately in the same clock edge. The synthesized circuit is the same as the one shown in Figure 6-5. Now let us consider the case where a variable is used before its assignment that occurs under the control of a clock.

```
VAR_FF: process
    variable TEMP: INTEGER range 0 to 15;
begin
    wait until CLK = '0';
    NEXT_STATE <= TEMP;
    TEMP := CURRENT_STATE;
end process;
```

In this case, falling-edge-triggered flip-flops are inferred for variable TEMP as well since its value needs to be saved between clock edges. The synthesized circuit is shown in Figure 6-6.

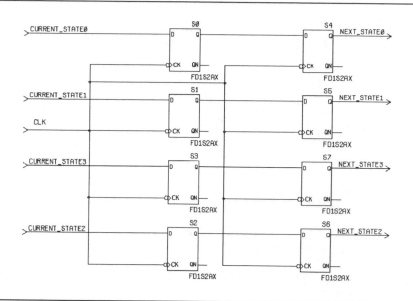

Figure 6-6 A variable is also inferred as a flip-flop.

6.5   Flip-flop with asynchronous preset and clear

To model a flip-flop with asynchronous preset and clear, a special form of the `if` statement is required. This is of the form:

> **if** *condition1* **then**
>   *-- Asynchronous-logic-1*
> **elsif** *condition2* **then**
>   *-- Asynchronous-logic-2*
> . . .
> **elsif** *clock_edge* **then**
>   *-- Synchronous-logic*
> **end if**;

where *clock_edge* is one of

> *clock_name = clock_value* **and** *clock_name*'EVENT
> *clock_name = clock_value* **and** (**not** *clock_name*'STABLE)
> RISING_EDGE (*clock_name*)
> FALLING_EDGE (*clock_name*)

where *clock_value* is either a logic-0 (to indicate a falling edge) or a logic-1 (to indicate a rising edge). The last two functions can be used only if the clock signal is of type STD_ULOGIC or STD_LOGIC.

The special if statement can have any number of elsif branches, with each branch describing asynchronous logic behavior except for the last elsif branch. The last elsif branch describes synchronous logic behavior and must have a clock edge as the branch condition. Note that this special if statement has no else branch. Here is an example of inferring a flip-flop with asynchronous preset and clear.

```
entity ASYNC_FLIP_FLOP is
    port (CLK, RESET, SET: in BIT;
            CURRENT_STATE: in INTEGER range 0 to 15;
            NEXT_STATE: out INTEGER range 0 to 15);
end ASYNC_FLIP_FLOP;

architecture INFER of ASYNC_FLIP_FLOP is
begin
    process (RESET, SET, CLK, CURRENT_STATE)
    begin
        if RESET = '0' then
            NEXT_STATE <= 12;            -- "1100" -- Stmt A
        elsif SET = '0' then
            NEXT_STATE <= 5;            -- "0101" -- Stmt B
        elsif CLK = '0' and CLK'EVENT then
            NEXT_STATE <= CURRENT_STATE; -- Stmt C
        end if;
    end process;
end INFER;
```

Since signal NEXT_STATE is assigned a value under the control of a clock edge (Stmt C) and it is also assigned asynchronously (Stmt A and B), a falling-edge-triggered flip-flop with asynchronous preset and clear is synthesized. This is shown in Figure 6-7. Note that four flip-flops are required. The first flip-flop (the leftmost bit of NEXT_STATE) has both asynchronous preset and clear terminals since it needs to be preset on signal RESET and cleared on signal SET. Similarly, the fourth flip-flop has both asynchronous preset and clear terminals since it needs to be preset on signal SET and cleared on signal RESET. The second flip-flop has only a preset terminal since a '1' is asynchronously assigned in both the conditions, while the third flip-flop has only a clear terminal since a '0' is assigned under both the conditions.

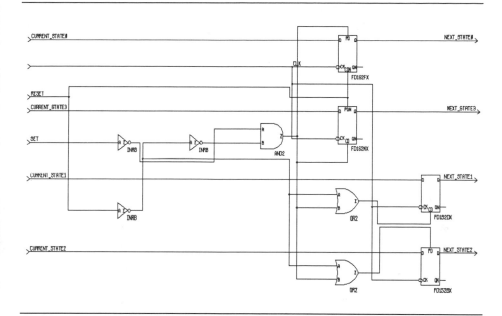

Figure 6-7 Flip-flops with asynchronous preset and clear.

6.6 Flip-flop with synchronous preset and clear

Let us first look at an example.

```
entity SYNC_FLIP_FLOP is
    port (CLK, RESET, SET: in BIT;
          CURRENT_STATE: in INTEGER range 0 to 15;
          NEXT_STATE: out INTEGER range 0 to 15);
end SYNC_FLIP_FLOP;

architecture IS_IT_SYNC of SYNC_FLIP_FLOP is
begin
    process
    begin
        wait until CLK = '0';

        if RESET = '0' then
            NEXT_STATE <= 12;          -- "1100"
        elsif SET = '0' then
            NEXT_STATE <= 5;           -- "0101"
        else
```

```
            NEXT_STATE <= CURRENT_STATE;
        end if;
      end process;
    end IS_IT_SYNC;
```

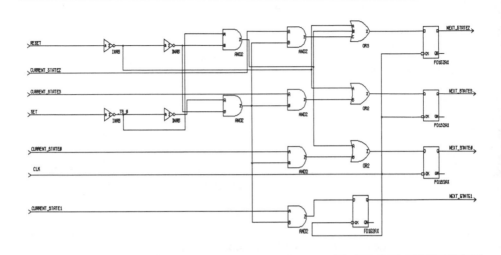

Figure 6-8 Not synchronous preset and clear flip-flop.

From this example, it appears that all the inputs to NEXT_STATE, the value 12, the value 5, and the signal CURRENT_STATE, should be multiplexed using appropriate select lines into the D-input of the inferred flip-flops for signal NEXT_STATE. This is shown in Figure 6-8. So then, how can we infer flip-flops with synchronous preset and clear? The ArchSyn synthesis system provides a solution for this by providing a special procedure called PRESET_CLEAR that is used to guide the synthesis tool to select a flip-flop with synchronous preset and clear.

```
        FF_SYNC: process
        begin
          wait until CLK = '0';

          if RESET = '0' then
            PRESET_CLEAR (NEXT_STATE, 12);   -- "1100"
          elsif SET = '0' then
            PRESET_CLEAR (NEXT_STATE, 5);    -- "0101"
          else
            NEXT_STATE <= CURRENT_STATE;
          end if;
        end process;
```

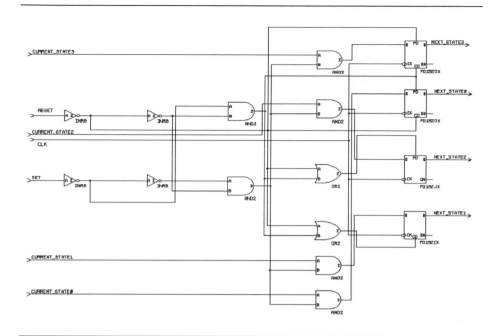

Figure 6-9 Flip-flops with synchronous preset and clear.

When this model is synthesized, the circuit of Figure 6-9 is obtained. Notice that the first and fourth flip-flops are synchronous preset and clear falling-edge-triggered flip-flops while the second flip-flop is a synchronous preset falling-edge-triggered flip-flop and the third flip-flop is a synchronous clear falling-edge-triggered flip-flop.

6.7   *Modeling a latch*

A level-sensitive flip-flop or a latch can be inferred by using an incompletely specified if statement or a case statement, that is, if a signal is not assigned a value in all branches of an if or a case statement, a latch is inferred for that signal. Here is an example.

```
entity LEVEL_FF is
    port (CLK: in BIT;
          CURRENT_STATE: in INTEGER range 0 to 15;
          NEXT_STATE: out INTEGER range 0 to 15);
    end;
```

```
architecture INFER of LEVEL_FF is
begin
  process (CLK, CURRENT_STATE)
  begin
    if CLK = '1' then
      NEXT_STATE <= CURRENT_STATE;
    end if;
  end process;
end INFER;
```

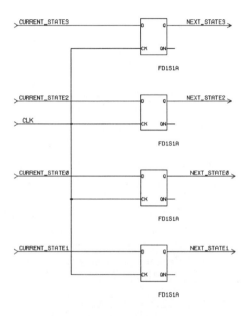

Figure 6-10 An incompletely specified condition infers a latch.

The signal NEXT_STATE is assigned a value only when signal CLK has the value '1'. If CLK is '0', NEXT_STATE retains its previous value, thus inferring a latch. The synthesized netlist is shown in Figure 6-10.

A variable is also inferred as a latch if it is incompletely assigned in a conditional statement (if statement or a case statement). This is shown in the following process. The synthesized circuit is the same as that shown in Figure 6-10.

```
NOT_ASSIGN: process (CLK, CURRENT_STATE)
   variable TEMP: INTEGER range 0 to 15;
begin
   if CLK = '1' then
      TEMP := CURRENT_STATE;
   end if;

   NEXT_STATE <= TEMP;
end process;
```

However, if a variable is defined and used within a conditional branch, no latch inference is necessary as shown in the following process. This is because the value of variable TEMP need not be saved between level changes of signal CLK.

```
NO_LATCH: process (CLK, CURRENT_STATE)
   variable TEMP: INTEGER range 0 to 15;
begin
   if CLK = '1' then
      TEMP := CURRENT_STATE;
      NEXT_STATE <= TEMP;
   end if;
end process;
```

If a variable is used before its definition, then a latch is inferred. Here is such a process. The synthesized circuit is shown in Figure 6-11.

```
-- Variable used before its definition:
VAR_LATCH: process (CLK, CURRENT_STATE)
   variable TEMP: INTEGER range 0 to 15;
begin
   if CLK = '1' then
      NEXT_STATE <= TEMP;
      TEMP := CURRENT_STATE;
   end if;
end process;
```

6.8   *Latch with asynchronous preset and clear*

If a signal is assigned in multiple branches of a conditional statement, bits that are '1' get assigned to the preset terminal while those with '0' get assigned to a latch with a clear terminal. This is shown in the following example. The synthesized netlist is shown in Figure 6-12.

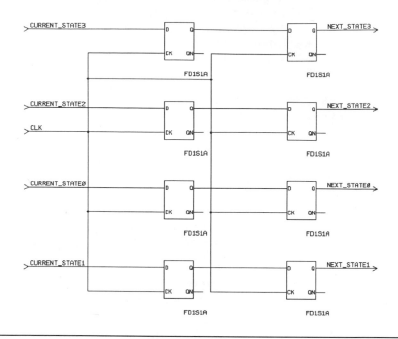

Figure 6-11 A variable used before being assigned in a conditional.

```
entity ASYNC_LATCH is
   port (CLK, RESET, SET: in BIT;
         CURRENT_STATE: in INTEGER range 0 to 15;
         NEXT_STATE: out INTEGER range 0 to 15);
end ASYNC_LATCH;

architecture ASYNC of ASYNC_LATCH is
begin
   process (RESET, SET, CLK, CURRENT_STATE)
   begin
      if RESET = '0' then
         NEXT_STATE <= 12;         -- "1100"
      elsif SET = '0' then
         NEXT_STATE <= 5;          -- "0101"
      elsif CLK = '0' then
         NEXT_STATE <= CURRENT_STATE;
      end if;
   end process;
end ASYNC;
```

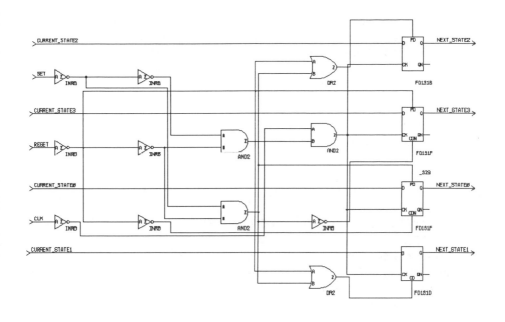

Figure 6-12 Latch with asynchronous preset and clear.

The first and the fourth latches have both preset and clear terminals since a '1' and a '0' are assigned under different conditions. The second latch has a preset terminal only while the third latch has an asynchronous clear terminal only.

6.9   Modeling a memory

A memory is best modeled as a component. Typically, synthesis tools are not efficient in designing a memory. More traditional techniques are usually used to build a memory. Once having built this component, it can then be instantiated in a synthesis model as a component using the component instantiation statement.

```
    . . .
        component ROM
          port (CK, OUT_ENA: in STD_LOGIC;
                ADDR: in STD_LOGIC_VECTOR (M–1 downto 0);
                Q, QN: out STD_LOGIC_VECTOR (N–1 downto 0));
```

```
end component;

signal CLK, ENA: STD_LOGIC;
signal ABUS: STD_LOGIC_VECTOR(M–1 downto 0);
signal DBUS: STD_LOGIC_VECTOR(N–1 downto 0);
begin
    R1: ROM (CK => CLK, OUT_ENA => ENA, ADDR => ABUS,
             Q => DBUS, QN => open);
    . . .
```

A register file can be modeled as a two-dimensional array of signals which can then be synthesized.

6.10   Using a pre-built component

There are times when a designer wants the synthesis tool to use a pre-built component instead of the one generated by the synthesis tool. In such a case, the best way is to instantiate the pre-built component as a component in the design.

Here is a 3-bit up-down counter that shows how a pre-built D-type flip-flop is used along with its remaining behavior. The key statements that are necessary to be added are the component instantiation statements and the component declaration. With such a model, a synthesis tool such as the ArchSyn system, retains the pre-built component in the synthesized design to achieve the desired result. This is shown in the synthesized netlist that appears in Figure 6-13.

```
library IEEE;
use IEEE.STD_LOGIC_1164.all;
entity UPC is
    port (CK, CUCD, PC: in STD_ULOGIC;
          Q0, Q1, Q2: out STD_ULOGIC);
end UPC;

architecture SPECIAL of UPC is
    signal QN0, QN1, QN2, BIT01, BIT11,
           BIT12, BIT13, BIT21: STD_ULOGIC;
    signal TQ0, TQ1: STD_ULOGIC;

    component SPECIAL_FF
        port (D, CLK, PRECLR: in STD_ULOGIC;
              Q, QBAR: out STD_ULOGIC);
```

```
            end component;
        begin
            Q0 <= TQ0;
            Q1 <= TQ1;

            BIT01 <= CUCD xor TQ0;
            BIT11 <= BIT01 xor QN1;
            BIT12 <= CUCD xor TQ1;
            BIT13 <= BIT01 or BIT12;
            BIT21 <= BIT13 xor QN2;

            LQ0: SPECIAL_FF port map (QN0, CK, PC, TQ0, QN0);
            LQ1: SPECIAL_FF port map (BIT11, CK, PC, TQ1, QN1);
            LQ2: SPECIAL_FF port map (BIT21, CK, PC, Q2, QN2);
        end SPECIAL;
```

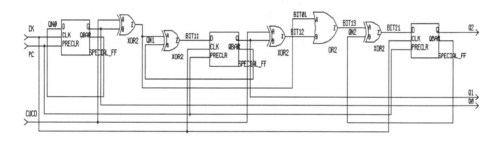

Figure 6-13 Using a special flip-flop.

6.11 *Writing boolean equations*

Boolean equations represent combinational logic. Boolean equations are
best represented using concurrent signal assignment statements. Here is
an example of a Gray code to binary code convertor using boolean equations. Figure 6-14 shows the synthesized logic.

A B C	Binary Code
0 0 0	0 0 0
0 0 1	0 0 1
0 1 1	0 1 0
0 1 0	0 1 1
1 1 0	1 0 0
1 1 1	1 0 1

```
1 0 1   1 1 0
1 0 0   1 1 1
```

entity GRAY_TO_BINARY **is**
   port (A, B, C: **in** BIT;
          BC0, BC1, BC2: **out** BIT);
end GRAY_TO_BINARY;

architecture BOOLEAN_LOGIC **of** GRAY_TO_BINARY **is**
   signal NOTA, NOTB, NOTC: BIT;
begin
   NOTC <= **not** C;
   NOTB <= **not** B;
   NOTA <= **not** A;

   BC0 <= (A **and** B **and** NOTC) **or** (A **and** B **and** C) **or**
          (A **and** NOTB **and** C) **or** (A **and** NOTB **and** NOTC);
   BC1 <= (NOTA **and** B **and** C) **or** (NOTA **and** B **and** NOTC) **or**
          (A **and** NOTB **and** C) **or** (A **and** NOTB **and** NOTC);
   BC2 <= (NOTA **and** NOTB **and** C) **or** (NOTA **and** B **and** NOTC) **or**
          (A **and** B **and** C) **or** (A **and** NOTB **and** NOTC);
end BOOLEAN_LOGIC;

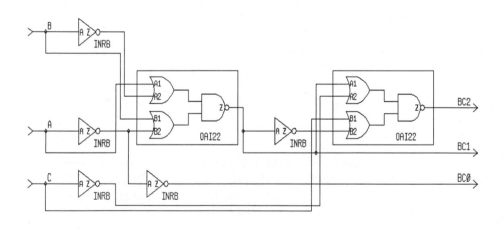

Figure 6-14 Gray to binary logic (after logic optimization).

   See the section on "Modeling combinational logic" for more examples.

6.12 Modeling a finite state machine

6.12.1 Moore FSM

In a Moore finite state machine, the output of the circuit is dependent only on the state of the machine and not on its inputs. This is described pictorially in Figure 6-15. Since the outputs are dependent only on the state, a good way to describe a Moore machine is to use a process statement with a `case` statement. The `case` statement is used to switch between the various states and the output logic for each state is described in the appropriate branch. Either an `if` statement with a clock expression can be used around the `case` statement or a `wait` statement that triggers on every clock edge can be used as the first statement within the process. This models the condition of a finite state machine going from state to state synchronously on every clock edge. The machine state itself could be implemented as a variable or as a signal.

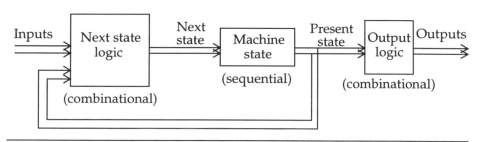

Figure 6-15 A Moore finite state machine.

Here is an example of a Moore finite state machine. A signal MOORE_STATE is used to model the machine state which can have either of the four states. The `wait` statement indicates that the state transitions occur synchronously on every rising clock edge.

```
library IEEE;
use IEEE.STD_LOGIC_1164.all;
entity MOORE is
   port (A, CLK: in STD_ULOGIC;
         Z: out STD_ULOGIC);
end MOORE;

architecture FSM_EXAMPLE of MOORE is
   type STATE_TYPE is (S0, S1, S2, S3);
   signal MOORE_STATE: STATE_TYPE;
```

```
begin
  process
  begin
    wait until CLK='1';

    case MOORE_STATE is
      when S0 =>
        Z <= '1';

        if A = '0' then
          MOORE_STATE <= S0;
        else
          MOORE_STATE <= S2;
        end if;
      when S1 =>
        Z <= '0';

        if A = '0' then
          MOORE_STATE <= S0;
        else
          MOORE_STATE <= S2;
        end if;
      when S2 =>
        Z <= '0';

        if A = '0' then
          MOORE_STATE <= S2;
        else
          MOORE_STATE <= S3;
        end if;
      when S3 =>
        Z <= '1';

        if A = '0' then
          MOORE_STATE <= S1;
        end if;
    end case;
  end process;
end FSM_EXAMPLE;
```

When this model is synthesized, three flip-flops are inferred; two to hold the value of the machine state (signal MOORE_STATE) and one for the output Z. The synthesized netlist is shown in Figure 6-16. States are encoded using sequential state assignment. This can be changed by using the attribute ENUM_TYPE_ENCODING in the ArchSyn synthesis system; such an example is shown in the next section.

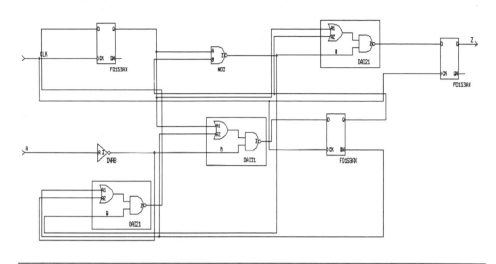

Figure 6-16 The synthesized netlist for the Moore FSM model.

6.12.2 Mealy FSM

In a Mealy finite state machine, the output is dependent both on the machine state as well as on the inputs to the finite state machine. This is shown pictorially in Figure 6-17. Notice that in this case, outputs can change asynchronously with respect to clock.

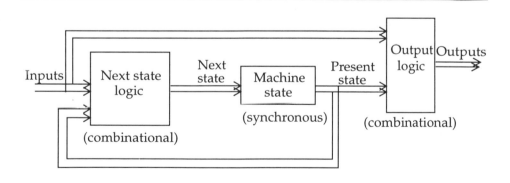

Figure 6-17 A Mealy finite state machine.

One of the best ways of describing a Mealy finite state machine is by using two processes, one for describing the synchronous logic, and one for describing the combinational logic (this includes both next state logic and output logic). It is necessary to do this since any changes on inputs directly affect the outputs of the process used to describe the combinational logic. Since there are two processes, the state of the machine has to be modeled using a signal.

Here is an example of a Mealy finite state machine. Signal MEALY_STATE holds the machine state, while signal NEXT_STATE is used to pass information from the combinational logic process to the sequential logic process. In this example, instead of using sequential state assignment, the state values are explicitly assigned using the attribute ENUM_TYPE_ENCODING; state ST0 has the value "1111", state ST1 has the value "1101", and so on.

```
package NEWPACK is
  type MEALY_TYPE is (ST0, ST1, ST2, ST3);
  attribute ENUM_TYPE_ENCODING: STRING;
  attribute ENUM_TYPE_ENCODING of MEALY_TYPE: type
    is "1111 1101 1001 1000";
end NEWPACK;

entity MEALY is
  port (A, CLK: in BIT;
        Z: out BIT);
end;

use WORK.NEWPACK.all;
architecture MEALY_FSM of MEALY is
  signal MEALY_STATE, NEXT_ST: MEALY_TYPE;
begin
  SEQ_LOGIC: process (CLK)
  begin
    if CLK = '1' and (not CLK'STABLE) then
      MEALY_STATE <= NEXT_ST;
    end if;
  end process;

  COMB_LOGIC: process (MEALY_STATE, A)
  begin
    case MEALY_STATE is
      when ST0 =>
        if A = '1' then
          Z <= '1';
          NEXT_ST <= ST3;
        else
          Z <= '0';
          NEXT_ST <= ST0; -- Assignment is redundant from simulation
```

```
            -- point of view but necessary for synthesis, else latches are inferred
            -- for signal NEXT_STATE.
          end if;
      when ST1 =>
        if A = '1' then
          Z <= '1';
          NEXT_ST <= ST0;
        else
          Z <= '0';
          NEXT_ST <= ST1;
        end if;
      when ST2 =>
        if A = '0' then
          Z <= '0';
          NEXT_ST <= ST2;
        else
          Z <= '1';
          NEXT_ST <= ST1;
        end if;
      when ST3 =>
        if A = '0' then
          Z <= '0';
          NEXT_ST <= ST2;
        else
          Z <= '0';
          NEXT_ST <= ST1;
        end if;
      end case;
    end process;
  end;
```

Four flip-flops are inferred to hold the value of the signal MEALY_STATE with the specified state assignment. Figure 6-18 shows the synthesized netlist for this example.

6.12.3 Encoding states

There are many ways to model the machine states of a finite state machine. Described here are some of the most common ones. The MOORE entity described earlier is used as an example in describing these encodings.

Using integer types

The simplest way is to assign integer values to states.

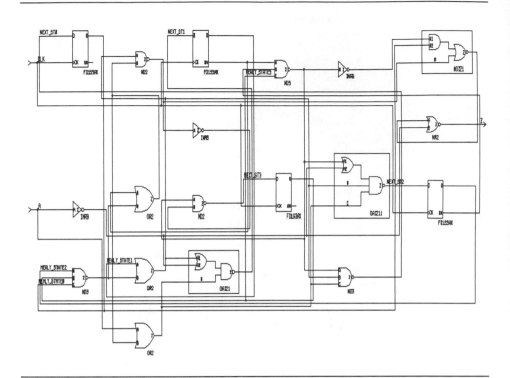

Figure 6-18 The synthesized netlist for the Mealy FSM example.

```
signal MOORE_STATE: INTEGER range 0 to 3;
. . .
case MOORE_STATE is
   when 0 => . . .
      MOORE_STATE <= 2;
      . . .
   when 1 =>
      . . .
end case;
```

Using constant declarations

Another option is to declare constants and use these in the case statement.

```
constant S0: NATURAL := 0;
constant S1: NATURAL := 1;
constant S2: NATURAL := 2;
```

```
constant S3: NATURAL := 3;

signal MOORE_STATE: INTEGER range 0 to 3;
. . .
case MOORE_STATE is
   when S0 => . . .
      MOORE_STATE <= S2;

      . . .
   when S1 =>

      . . .
end case;
```

The advantage of this approach is that the state encodings are described explicitly in one place and can be changed easily. If either the constant declarations or the integer values are used directly, the ArchSyn system generates the minimum number of bits needed to encode the integer value. In the above example, only two bits are needed for state encoding since the maximum integer value is 3.

What if a different encoding needs to be specified, for example, 1-shift encoding? This can be done by describing each state as a vector of bits.

```
constant S0: STD_LOGIC_VECTOR := "000";
constant S1: STD_LOGIC_VECTOR := "001";
constant S2: STD_LOGIC_VECTOR := "010";
constant S3: STD_LOGIC_VECTOR := "100";

signal MOORE_STATE: STD_LOGIC_VECTOR (0 to 2);
. . .
case MOORE_STATE is
   when S0 => . . .
      MOORE_STATE <= S2;

      . . .
   when S1 =>

      . . .
end case;
```

In this case, the number of bits required for state encoding is dictated by the number of bits in the constant which in this example is 3 bits.

Using enumeration types

VHDL also provides enumeration types which can very conveniently be used in describing the states of a finite state machine.

```
type FSM_STATES is (S0, S1, S2, S3);

signal MOORE_STATE: FSM_STATES;
. . .
case MOORE_STATE is
  when S0 => . . .
    MOORE_STATE <= S2;
    . . .
  when S1 =>
    . . .
end case;
```

Notice that in this case, no explicit encoding for the enumeration types is specified. So what is the value used for each state? In the ArchSyn synthesis system, each enumeration literal is encoded to correspond to its position number in the enumeration type, that is, literal S0 is encoded with value 0, S1 with 1, S2 with 2 and S3 with 3. Thus two bits will be used for holding the state value.

How can this encoding be changed? This can be done using the ENUM_TYPE_ENCODING attribute provided in the ArchSyn synthesis system. Using this attribute, each state is explicitly encoded as a bit string. Here is an example.

```
type FSM_STATES is (S0, S1, S2, S3);

signal MOORE_STATE: FSM_STATES;

attribute ENUM_TYPE_ENCODING: STRING;
attribute ENUM_TYPE_ENCODING of FSM_STATES:
    type is "000 001 011 111";
. . .
case MOORE_STATE is
  when S0 => . . .
    MOORE_STATE <= S2;
    . . .
  when S1 =>
    . . .
end case;
```

Since each state is encoded as 3 bits, three state flip-flops are inferred for this example.

The above techniques show how states can be explicitly or implicitly encoded. Other synthesis systems may provide an option for performing automated state assignment.

6.13 Modeling an universal shift register

Here is a synthesis model of a 3-bit universal shift register. The universal shift register performs the following functions:

i.   hold value

ii. shift left

iii. shift right

iv. load value

This universal register can be used as a serial-in, serial-out shift register, parallel-in, serial-out shift register, serial-in, parallel-out shift register, and as a parallel-in, parallel-out shift register. Here is the state table for the 3-bit universal shift register.

Function	Inputs (S0 S1)		Next state (QA QB QC)		
Hold	0	0	QA	QB	QC
Shift left	0	1	QB	QC	RIN
Shift right	1	0	LIN	QA	QB
Load	1	1	A	B	C

The synthesis model follows. The synthesized netlist is shown in Figure 6-19.

```
library IEEE;
use IEEE.STD_LOGIC_1164.all;
entity UNIV_SHIFT_REG is
    port (CLK, CLR, LIN, RIN, S0, S1, A, B, C: in STD_ULOGIC;
          QA, QB, QC: buffer STD_ULOGIC);
end UNIV_SHIFT_REG;

architecture CASE_EXAMPLE of UNIV_SHIFT_REG is
begin
    process (CLK, CLR, LIN, RIN, S0, S1, A, B, C)
       subtype TWO_BIT is STD_ULOGIC_VECTOR (0 to 1);
    begin
```

```
                    if CLR = '0' then
                       QA <= '0';
                       QB <= '0';
                       QC <= '0';
                    elsif RISING_EDGE (CLK) then
                       case TWO_BIT'(S0 & S1)) is
                          when "00" =>
                             null;
                          when "01" =>
                             QA <= QB;
                             QB <= QC;
                             QC <= RIN;
                          when "10" =>
                             QA <= LIN;
                             QB <= QA;
                             QC <= QB;
                          when "11" =>
                             QA <= A;
                             QB <= B;
                             QC <= C;
                          when others =>
                             null;
                       end case;
                    end if;
                 end process;
              end CASE_EXAMPLE;
```

6.14 Modeling an ALU

6.14.1 A generic ALU

Here is an example of a generic N-bit arithmetic-logic-unit that performs
an exclusive-or, less than, and an increment-by-1 operation.

```
              library IEEE, SYNTH;
              use IEEE.STD_LOGIC_1164.all;
              use SYNTH.STD_LOGIC_ARITH.all;
              entity FDS_ALU is
                 generic (NBITS: POSITIVE);
                 port (A: in STD_LOGIC_VECTOR (NBITS−1 downto 0);
                       B: in STD_LOGIC_VECTOR (NBITS−1 downto 0);
                       SEL: in STD_LOGIC_VECTOR(3 downto 0);
                       CMP: out STD_LOGIC;
                       D: out STD_LOGIC_VECTOR (NBITS−1 downto 0));
```

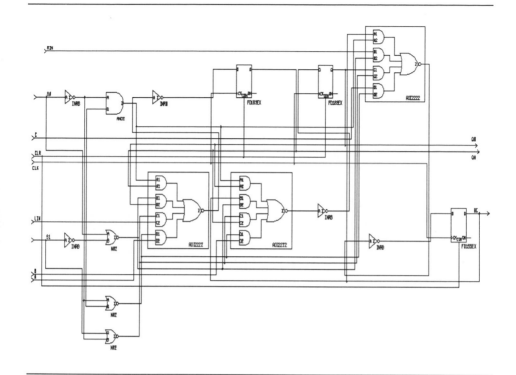

Figure 6-19 A 3-bit universal shift register.

end FDS_ALU;

architecture BEHAVIOR **of** FDS_ALU **is**
    constant OP_XOR: STD_LOGIC_VECTOR := "1111";
    constant OP_INCRA: STD_LOGIC_VECTOR := "1000";
    constant OP_LT: STD_LOGIC_VECTOR := "0011";
begin
    ALU_PROCESS: -- Process label.
    process (A, B, SEL)
    begin
        case SEL **is**
            when OP_INCRA =>
                D <= STD_LOGIC_VECTOR(UNSIGNED(A) + 1);
                CMP <= 'X';
            when OP_XOR =>
                D <= A **xor** B;
                CMP <= 'X';
            when OP_LT =>
                if A < B **then**

```
            CMP <= '1';
        else
            CMP <= '0';
        end if;

        D <= (others => 'X');
    when others =>  -- Invalid selector input.
        CMP <= 'X' ;
        D <= (others => 'X');
    end case;
  end process ALU_PROCESS;
end BEHAVIOR;
```

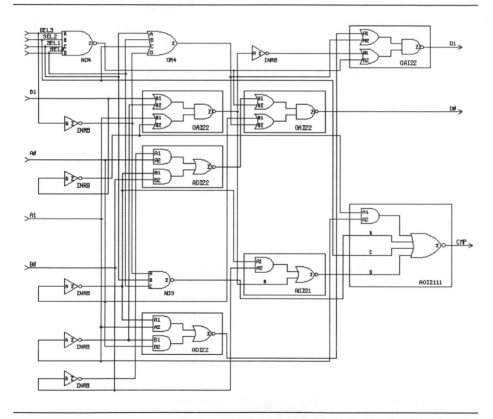

Figure 6-20 A 2-bit ALU.

The generic ALU can be synthesized by specifying the value of the generic when it is instantiated. This is shown in the following example for a 2-bit ALU. The synthesized netlist is shown in Figure 6-20.

```
library IEEE;
use IEEE.STD_LOGIC_1164.all;
entity ALU2BIT is
  port (A: in STD_LOGIC_VECTOR (NBITS–1 downto 0);
        B: in STD_LOGIC_VECTOR (NBITS–1 downto 0);
        SEL: in STD_LOGIC_VECTOR (3 downto 0);
        CMP: out STD_LOGIC;
        D: out STD_LOGIC_VECTOR (NBITS–1 downto 0));
end ALU2BIT;

architecture PART of ALU2BIT is
  component FDS_ALU
    generic (NBITS: POSITIVE);
    port (A: in STD_LOGIC_VECTOR (NBITS–1 downto 0);
          B: in STD_LOGIC_VECTOR (NBITS–1 downto 0);
          SEL: in STD_LOGIC_VECTOR (3 downto 0);
          CMP: out STD_LOGIC;
          D: out STD_LOGIC_VECTOR (NBITS–1 downto 0));
  end component;
begin
  NUM: FDS_ALU
          generic map (BITS => 2)
          port map (A, B, SEL, CMP, D);
end PART;
```

6.14.2 A simple ALU

Here is a model of a simple arithmetic-logic-unit. This logic unit performs four functions: add, nand, greater-than and xor of the signed operands. A selected signal assignment statement is used to model the arithmetic-logic-unit. Figure 6-21 shows the synthesized netlist.

```
package UTILS is
  type OP_TYPE is (ADD_OP, NAND_OP, GT_OP, XOR_OP);
end;

library IEEE, SYNTH;
use IEEE.STD_LOGIC_1164.all;
use SYNTH.STD_LOGIC_ARITH.all, WORK.UTILS.all;
entity CUSTOM_ALU is
  generic (NBITS: POSITIVE);
  port (A, B: in SIGNED (NBITS–1 downto 0);
        OP_CODE: in OP_TYPE;
        ZDATA: out SIGNED (NBITS–1 downto 0);
        ZCOMP: out BOOLEAN);
end CUSTOM_ALU;
```

```
architecture TEST of CUSTOM_ALU is
begin
  with OP_CODE select
    ZDATA <= A + B when ADD_OP,
             A nand B when NAND_OP,
             A xor B when XOR_OP,
             (others => 'X') when others;

  with OP_CODE select
    ZCOMP <= A > B when GT_OP,
             FALSE when others;
end TEST;
```

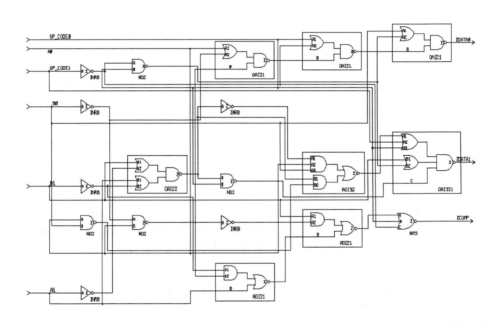

Figure 6-21 A 2-bit custom ALU.

6.15 Modeling a counter

6.15.1 Ripple counter

Here is a model for a generic N-bit binary ripple up-down counter with synchronous preset and preclear controls. The counting is synchronized to the rising edge of a clock. Figure 6-22 shows the synthesized netlist of a 2-bit ripple counter.

```
library IEEE, SYNTH;
use IEEE.STD_LOGIC_1164.all;
use SYNTH.STD_LOGIC_ARITH.all;
entity RIPPLE_COUNTER is
  generic (NBITS: POSITIVE);
  port (CK, CUCD, PC, CTLD: in STD_LOGIC;
        PI: in STD_LOGIC_VECTOR(0 to NBITS-1);
        Q: out STD_LOGIC_VECTOR(0 to NBITS-1);
        QN: out STD_LOGIC_VECTOR(0 to NBITS-1));
end RIPPLE_COUNTER;

architecture BEHAVIOR of RIPPLE_COUNTER is
begin
  COUNTER_PROCESS:
  process (CK)
    variable CNTR_VALUE: UNSIGNED(NBITS-1 downto 0);
  begin
    if RISING_EDGE(CK) then  -- Rising-edge triggered.
      if PC = '1' then              -- Check preclear:
        CNTR_VALUE := (others => '0');
      else                          -- Actual counting or loading process:
        if CTLD = '0' then          -- Parallel loading.
          CNTR_VALUE := UNSIGNED(PI);
        else                        -- Beginning of counting part:
          if CUCD = '1' then  -- Count up.
            CNTR_VALUE := CNTR_VALUE + 1;
          else                -- Count down.
            CNTR_VALUE := CNTR_VALUE - 1;
          end if;      -- The end of counting part.
        end if;      -- The end of parallel-loading routine.
      end if;        -- The end of check input.
    end if;          -- End of clock trigger.


  -- Output assignment:
  Q <= STD_LOGIC_VECTOR(CNTR_VALUE);
  QN <= not STD_LOGIC_VECTOR(CNTR_VALUE);
```

```
    end process COUNTER_PROCESS;
    end BEHAVIOR;
```

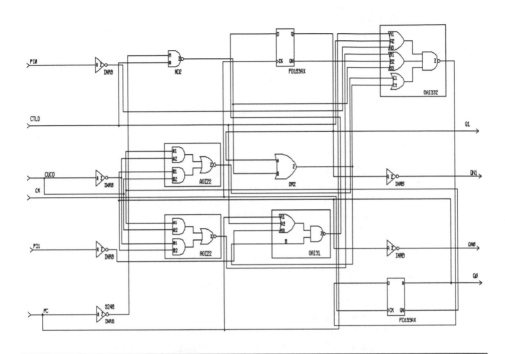

Figure 6-22 A 2-bit up-down, loadable, clearable ripple counter.

6.15.2 Modulo-N counter

Here is a model of a modulo-N binary up-counter. This counter has only a synchronous preclear control and all transitions occur on the rising clock edge. Figure 6-23 shows the synthesized netlist for a modulo-3 binary counter.

```
-- Number of bits in counter: NBITS
-- Modulo: UPTO
library IEEE, SYNTH;
use IEEE.STD_LOGIC_1164.all;
use SYNTH.STD_LOGIC_ARITH.all;
entity MODULO_N is
    generic (NBITS, UPTO: POSITIVE);
```

```
        port (CK, PC: in STD_LOGIC;
              PI: in STD_LOGIC_VECTOR(0 to NBITS-1);
              Q: out STD_LOGIC_VECTOR(0 to NBITS-1);
              QN: out STD_LOGIC_VECTOR(0 to NBITS-1));
        end MODULO_N;

        architecture BEHAVIOR of MODULO_N is
        begin
          process (CK)
            variable CNTR_VALUE: UNSIGNED(NBITS-1 downto 0);
          begin
            if RISING_EDGE(CK) then  -- Rising-edge trigger.
              if PC = '1' then            -- Check preclear:
                CNTR_VALUE := (others => '0');
              else                        -- Counting part:
                CNTR_VALUE := (CNTR_VALUE + 1) mod UPTO;
              end if;        -- The end of check input.
            end if;          -- End of clock trigger.

            -- Output assignment:
            Q <= STD_LOGIC_VECTOR (CNTR_VALUE);
            QN <= not STD_LOGIC_VECTOR (CNTR_VALUE);
          end process;
        end BEHAVIOR;
```

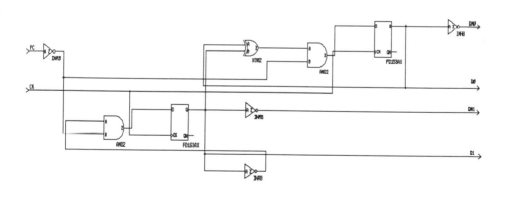

Figure 6-23 A modulo-3 binary counter.

6.15.3 Johnson counter

A Johnson counter is a shift-type counter. Here is an example of a 3-bit Johnson counter stream:

```
000
001
011
111
110
100
000
```

The key to modeling a Johnson counter is to note that if the most significant bit (the leftmost bit) of the counter is a '1', then a '0' has to be shifted in from right; if the most significant bit is a '0', then a '1' has to be shifted in from the right. Here is the model for a generic N-bit Johnson counter with an asynchronous preclear control. Figure 6-24 shows the synthesized netlist for a 3-bit Johnson counter.

```
library IEEE;
use IEEE.STD_LOGIC_1164.all;
entity JOHNSON_COUNTER is
    generic (NBITS: POSITIVE);
    port (CK, PC: in STD_LOGIC;
          Q: out STD_LOGIC_VECTOR (0 to NBITS–1));
end JOHNSON_COUNTER;

architecture BEHAVIOR of JOHNSON_COUNTER is
begin
    process (CK, PC)
        variable CNTR_VALUE: STD_LOGIC_VECTOR (0 to NBITS–1);
    begin
        if PC = '0' then                     -- Asynchronous preclear.
            CNTR_VALUE := (others => '0');
        elsif FALLING_EDGE (CK) then  -- Falling-edge trigger.
            if CNTR_VALUE(0) = '0' then
                CNTR_VALUE := CNTR_VALUE(1 to NBITS–1) & '1';
            else
                CNTR_VALUE := CNTR_VALUE(1 to NBITS–1) & '0';
            end if;
        end if;

        Q <= CNTR_VALUE;
    end process;
end BEHAVIOR;
```

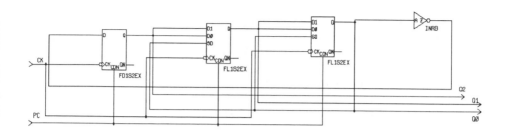

Figure 6-24 A 3-bit Johnson counter.

6.15.4 Gray counter

A Gray counter is basically a binary counter with the following conversion logic:

i.   The first Gray bit (the leftmost bit) is the same as the first binary bit.

ii. Exclusive-or each pair of adjacent bits to get the next Gray bit.

For example, a binary count of "1100" corresponds to a Gray count of "1010". Here is the VHDL model for a generic N-bit Gray up-counter with synchronous preclear. The synthesized netlist for a 3-bit Gray counter is shown in Figure 6-25.

```
library IEEE, SYNTH;
use IEEE.STD_LOGIC_1164.all;
use SYNTH.STD_LOGIC_ARITH.all;
entity GRAY_COUNTER is
    generic (NBITS: POSITIVE);
    port (CK, PC: in STD_LOGIC;
            Q: out STD_LOGIC_VECTOR(0 to NBITS−1);
            QN: out STD_LOGIC_VECTOR(0 to NBITS−1));
end GRAY_COUNTER;

architecture BEHAVIOR of GRAY_COUNTER is
begin
    COUNTER_PROCESS:
    process (CK)
        variable CNTR_VALUE: UNSIGNED(0 to NBITS−1);
        variable GRAY_CNT: STD_LOGIC_VECTOR (0 to NBITS−1);
    begin
```

```
if RISING_EDGE(CK) then   -- Rising-edge trigger.
   if PC = '1' then            -- Check preclear:
      CNTR_VALUE := (others => '0');
   else
      CNTR_VALUE := CNTR_VALUE + 1;
   end if;  -- The end of check input.
end if;  -- End of clock trigger.

-- Output assignment: convert from binary to Gray:
GRAY_CNT(0) := CNTR_VALUE(0);

for K in 1 to NBITS–1 loop
   GRAY_CNT (K) := CNTR_VALUE(K–1) xor CNTR_VALUE(K);
end loop;

Q <= GRAY_CNT;
QN <= not GRAY_CNT;
  end process COUNTER_PROCESS;
end BEHAVIOR;
```

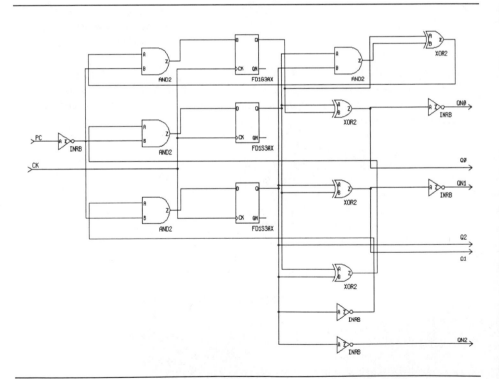

Figure 6-25 A 3-bit Gray counter.

6.16 Modeling a generic adder

Here is a model for a generic N-bit adder with carry input and output. The rightmost bit is the most significant bit. Figure 6-26 shows the synthesized netlist for a 3-bit adder with carry-in and carry-out.

```
library IEEE;
use IEEE.STD_LOGIC_1164.all;
entity ADD_CI_CO is
   generic (NBITS: POSITIVE);
   port (A: in STD_LOGIC_VECTOR (1 to NBITS);
         B: in STD_LOGIC_VECTOR(1 to NBITS);
         CI: in STD_LOGIC;
         CO: out STD_LOGIC;
         S: out STD_LOGIC_VECTOR(1 to NBITS));
end ADD_CI_CO;

architecture BEHAVIOR of ADD_CI_CO is
begin
   ADDER_PROCESS:
   process (A, B, CI)
      variable C: STD_LOGIC_VECTOR(1 to NBITS+1);
      variable STEMP: STD_LOGIC_VECTOR(1 to NBITS);
   begin
      -- Initialize the carry array and the sum.
      C := (others => '0');
      STEMP := (others => '0');

      -- Carry input.
      C(1) := CI;

      -- Actual processing.
      for I in A'RANGE loop
         STEMP(I) := (A(I) xor B(I)) xor C(I);
         C(I+1) := (A(I) and B(I)) or (A(I) and C(I)) or (B(I) and C(I));
      end loop;

      CO <= C(NBITS);
      S <= STEMP;
   end process ADDER_PROCES;
end BEHAVIOR;
```

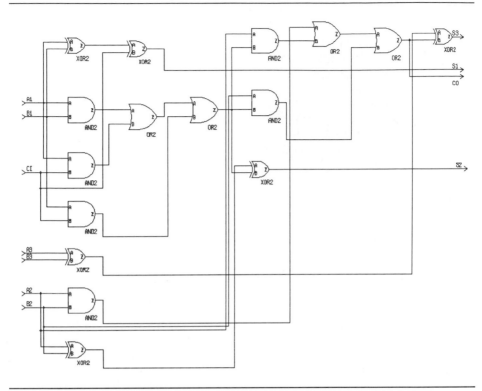

Figure 6-26 A 3-bit adder with carry-in and carry-out.

6.17 *Modeling a generic comparator*

Here is a model for a generic N-bit binary comparator. The input vectors are treated as unsigned quantities and a numerical comparison is made. Figure 6-27 shows the synthesized netlist for a 2-bit comparator.

```
library IEEE, SYNTH;
use IEEE.STD_LOGIC_1164.all;
use SYNTH.STD_LOGIC_ARITH.all;
entity COMPARATOR is
    generic (NBITS: POSITIVE);
    port (A: in STD_LOGIC_VECTOR(0 to NBITS−1);
          B: in STD_LOGIC_VECTOR(0 to NBITS−1);
          EQ, GT, LT, NE, GE, LE: out STD_LOGIC);
end COMPARATOR;
```

```
architecture BEHAVIOR of COMPARATOR is
begin
  COMPARATOR_PROCESS:
  process (A,B)
  begin
    if UNSIGNED(A) > UNSIGNED(B) then
        EQ <= '0';
        GT <= '1';
        LT <= '0';
        NE <= '1';
        GE <= '1';
        LE <= '0';
    elsif UNSIGNED(A) < UNSIGNED(B) then
        EQ <= '0';
        GT <= '0';
        LT <= '1';
        NE <= '1';
        GE <= '0';
        LE <= '1';
    else
        EQ <= '1';
        GT <= '0';
        LT <= '0';
        NE <= '0';
        GE <= '1';
        LE <= '1';
    end if;
  end process COMPARATOR_PROCESS;
end BEHAVIOR;
```

6.18 Modeling a generic decoder

6.18.1 A simple decoder

Here is an example of a simple 2-by-4 decoder circuit. This is a combinational circuit modeled purely using concurrent signal assignment statements. The delays specified with the assignment statements are typically ignored by a synthesis system; this is the case with the ArchSyn synthesis system. Figure 6-28 shows the synthesized netlist.

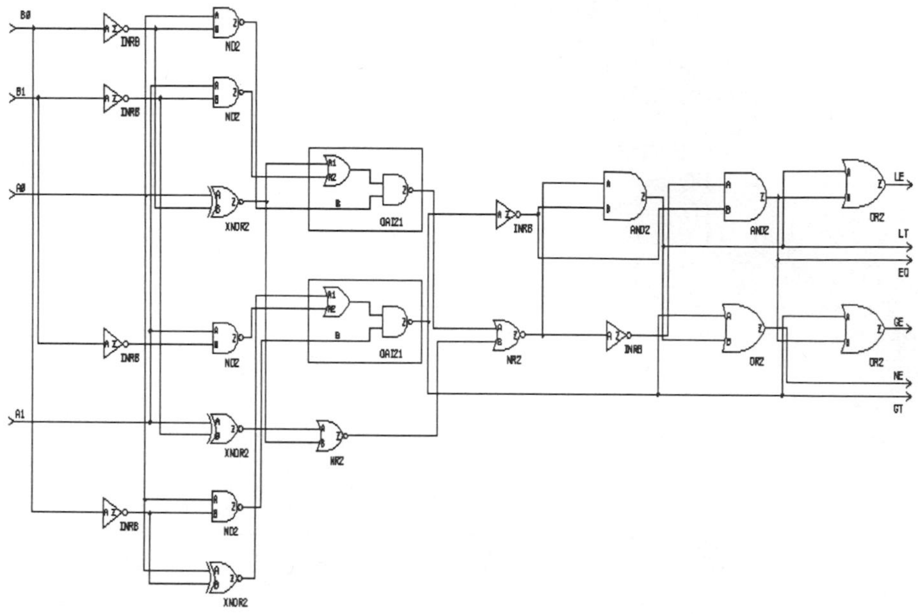

Figure 6-27 A 2-bit comparator.

```
library IEEE;
use IEEE.STD_LOGIC_1164.all;
entity DEC is
    port (A, B, ENABLE: in STD_ULOGIC;
        Z0, Z1, Z2, Z3: out STD_ULOGIC);
end DEC;

architecture DEC_DF of DEC is
    signal ABAR, BBAR: STD_ULOGIC;
begin
    ABAR <= not A after 1 ns;
    BBAR <= not B after 1 ns;
    Z0 <= not (ENABLE and ABAR and BBAR) after 2 ns;
    Z1 <= not (ENABLE and ABAR and B) after 2 ns;
    Z2 <= not (ENABLE and A and BBAR) after 2 ns;
    Z3 <= not (ENABLE and A and B) after 2 ns;
end DEC_DF;
```

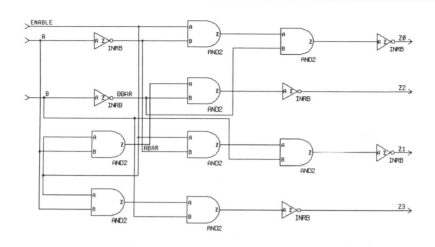

Figure 6-28 A simple 2-by-4 decoder.

6.18.2 Binary decoder

Here is a model of a generic N-bit binary decoder. The synthesized circuit
for a 2-bit binary decoder is shown in Figure 6-29.

```
library IEEE;
use IEEE.STD_LOGIC_1164.all;
entity BINARY_DECODER is
   generic (SBITS: POSITIVE);
   port (S: in STD_LOGIC_VECTOR(0 to SBITS−1);
         Y: out STD_LOGIC_VECTOR(0 to 2**SBITS−1));
end BINARY_DECODER;

architecture BEHAVIOR of BINARY_DECODER is
begin
   DECODER_PROCESS:
   process (S)
      variable ADDRESS: INTEGER;
   begin
      ADDRESS := TO_INTEGER(UNSIGNED(S));

      for K in Y'RANGE loop
         if K = ADDRESS  then
            Y(K) <= '1';
         else
            Y(K) <= '0';
         end if;
```

```
        end loop;
      end process DECODER_PROCESS;
    end BEHAVIOR;
```

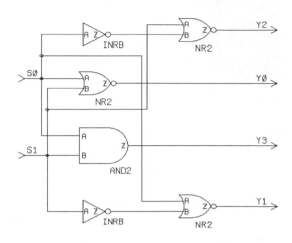

Figure 6-29 A 2-bit binary decoder.

6.18.3 Johnson decoder

Here is a model of a generic N-bit Johnson decoder with an enable control. Figure 6-30 shows the synthesized netlist for a 3-bit Johnson decoder.

```
    library IEEE;
    use IEEE.STD_LOGIC_1164.all;
    entity JOHNSON_DECODER is
        generic (NBITS: POSITIVE);
        port (S: in STD_LOGIC_VECTOR(0 to NBITS−1);
              EN: in STD_LOGIC;
              Y: out STD_LOGIC_VECTOR(0 to 2*NBITS−1));
    end JOHNSON_DECODER;

    architecture BEHAVIOR of JOHNSON_DECODER is
    begin
        DECODER_PROCESS:
        process (S, EN)
            variable ADDRESS: INTEGER range 0 to 2*NBITS−1;
        begin
            if EN = '1' then -- Enable signal.
                -- Calculate the output address.
                ADDRESS := 0;
```

```
if (S(0) = S(NBITS–1)) or (S(0) = '1' and S(NBITS–1) = '0')  then
  -- First half of JOHNSON code.
  for K in 0 to NBITS–1 loop
    if S(K) = '1' then
      ADDRESS := ADDRESS + 1;
    end if;
  end loop;
else                   -- Second half of JOHNSON code.
  for K in 0 to NBITS–1 loop
    if S(K) = '0' then
      ADDRESS := ADDRESS + 1;
    end if;
  end loop;

  ADDRESS := NBITS + ADDRESS;
end if;

Y <= (others => '0');
Y(ADDRESS) <= '1';
elsif EN = '0' then          -- Enable signal is inactive.
  Y <= (others => '0');
else                         -- Enable signal is unknown.
  Y <= (others => 'X');
end if;                      -- End of enable.
end process DECODER_PROCESS;
end BEHAVIOR;
```

6.19 Modeling a multiplexer

6.19.1 A simple multiplexer

Here is a model of a 4-by-1 multiplexer circuit. In this case, a process statement has been used to model the combinational logic. Figure 6-31 shows the synthesized netlist.

```
library IEEE;
use IEEE.STD_LOGIC_1164.all;
entity MUX4x1 is
  port (D: in STD_LOGIC_VECTOR(0 to 3);
        S: in STD_LOGIC_VECTOR(0 to 1);
        Z: out STD_LOGIC);
end MUX4x1;
```

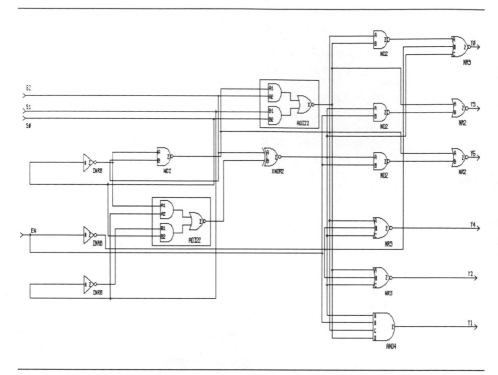

Figure 6-30 A 3-bit Johnson decoder.

```
architecture SEQ_EX of MUX4x1 is
begin
    process (D, S)
    begin
        case S is
            when "00" =>
                Z <= D(0);
            when "01" =>
                Z <= D(1);
            when "10" =>
                Z <= D(2);
            when "11" =>
                Z <= D(3);
            when others =>
                Z <= 'X';
        end case;
    end process;
end SEQ_EX;
```

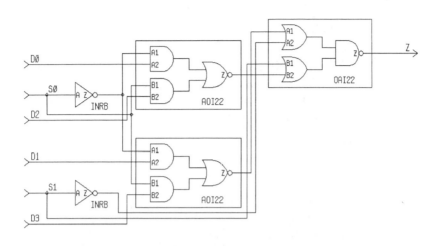

Figure 6-31 A 4-by-1 multiplexer.

An alternate way of modeling the simple multiplexer is shown in the following architecture body. The synthesized netlist is identical to the one shown in Figure 6-31.

```
architecture SIMPLER of MUX4x1 is
begin
    Z <= D(TO_INTEGER(UNSIGNED(S)));
end SIMPLER;
```

6.19.2 A generic multiplexer

Here is a model of a generic multiplexer. The number of bits per word and the number of words in the multiplexer are modeled as constants in a package. The multiplexer has inverted select lines, an enable signal, and the select lines are non-encoded. The inverted outputs are also provided. The synthesized netlist of a 2-by-2 (2 words of 2 bits per word) multiplexer is shown in Figure 6-32.

```
library IEEE;
use IEEE.STD_LOGIC_1164.all;
package TYPES is
    constant NBITS: NATURAL := 2;
    constant WORDS: NATURAL := 2;
    type MUX_TYPE is array (WORDS–1 downto 0) of
        STD_LOGIC_VECTOR(NBITS–1 downto 0);
end;
```

```vhdl
use WORK.TYPES.all;
library IEEE;
use IEEE.STD_LOGIC_1164.all;
entity BINARY_MULTIPLEXER is
  port (DB: in MUX_TYPE;
       S: in STD_LOGIC_VECTOR(WORDS-1 downto 0);
       EN: in STD_LOGIC;
       Y: out STD_LOGIC_VECTOR(NBITS-1 downto 0);
       YN: out STD_LOGIC_VECTOR(NBITS-1 downto 0));
end BINARY_MULTIPLEXER;

architecture BEHAVIOR of BINARY_MULTIPLEXER is
begin
  MULTIPLEXER_PROCESS:
  process (DB, S, EN)
    variable INVALID: INTEGER;
    variable SELECTOR_VALUE: INTEGER;
    variable Y_TEMP: STD_LOGIC_VECTOR(NBITS-1 downto 0);
  begin
    if EN = '1' then                -- Enable signal.
      -- Calculate the selector value.
      SELECTOR_VALUE := -1;

      for M in 0 to WORDS-1 loop
        if S(M) = '0' then
          if SELECTOR_VALUE = -1 then
            SELECTOR_VALUE := M;
          else
            INVALID := 1;
            exit;
          end if;
        end if;
      end loop;

      if SELECTOR_VALUE = -1 then -- No selector line is active.
        INVALID := 1;
      end if;

      -- Selection of input for output.
      if INVALID = 1 then
        Y <= (others => 'X');
        YN <= (others => 'X');
      else
        Y_TEMP := DB(SELECTOR_VALUE);
        Y <= Y_TEMP;
        YN <= not Y_TEMP;
```

```
                        end if;
                    elsif EN = '0' then                -- When enable is inactive.
                        Y <= (others => 'Z');
                        YN <= (others => 'Z');
                    else                               -- When enable is unknown.
                        Y <= (others => 'X');
                        YN <= (others => 'X');
                    end if;
                end process MULTIPLEXER_PROCESS;
            end BEHAVIOR;
```

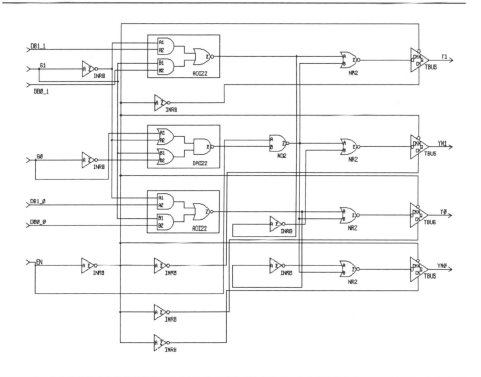

Figure 6-32 A 2-by-2 binary multiplexer.

6.20 Modeling a generic parity circuit

Here is a model of a generic N-bit parity detector circuit. The model provides both an odd parity and an even parity output. Figure 6-33 shows the
synthesized netlist of a 4-bit parity detector.

```
library IEEE;
use IEEE.STD_LOGIC_1164.all;
entity PARITY is
   generic (NBITS: POSITIVE);
   port (D: in STD_LOGIC_VECTOR(NBITS-1 downto 0);
         ODF: out STD_LOGIC;
         EDF: out STD_LOGIC);
end PARITY;

architecture BEHAVIOR of PARITY is
begin
   PARITY_PROCESS:
   process (D)
      variable NO_OF_ONES: INTEGER range 0 to NBITS;
   begin
      -- Initialization.
      NO_OF_ONES := 0;

      -- Count the number of ones in the input
      COUNT_ONES:
      for M in D'RANGE loop
         if D(M) = '1' then
            NO_OF_ONES := NO_OF_ONES + 1;
         end if;
      end loop COUNT_ONES;

      -- Parity detector.
      if (NO_OF_ONES rem 2) = 0 then
         ODF <= '0';
         EDF <= '1';
      else
         ODF <= '1';
         EDF <= '0';
      end if;
   end process PARITY_PROCESS;
end BEHAVIOR;
```

6.21 Modeling a tri-state gate

A tri-state gate is modeled by assigning a high-impedance value (Z) to a
signal under the control of a condition. Here is an example.

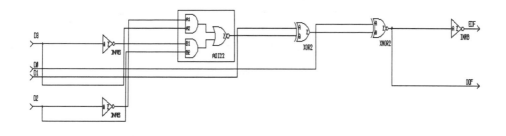

Figure 6-33 A 4-bit parity detector.

```
library IEEE;
use IEEE.STD_LOGIC_1164.all;
entity TRISTATE is
   port (READ_STATE: in BOOLEAN;
         CPU_BUS: in STD_LOGIC_VECTOR(0 to 3);
         MAIN_BUS: out STD_LOGIC_VECTOR (0 to 3));
end TRISTATE;

architecture BANK of TRISTATE is
begin
   process (READ_STATE, CPU_BUS)
   begin
      if READ_STATE then           -- If CPU in READ state.
         MAIN_BUS <= (others => 'Z');
      else
         MAIN_BUS <= CPU_BUS;
      end if;
   end process;
end BANK;
```

The synthesized netlist is shown in Figure 6-34. The signal MAIN_BUS is tristate'ed as long as READ_STATE is true. If READ_STATE is false, the value of CPU_BUS is assigned to MAIN_BUS.

6.22 A count three 1's model

Here is a model that detects three 1's in an input data stream appearing on signal DATA. This signal is checked on every falling clock edge. If three consecutive 1's are found on the input, the output is set to a '1', else it is set to a '0'.

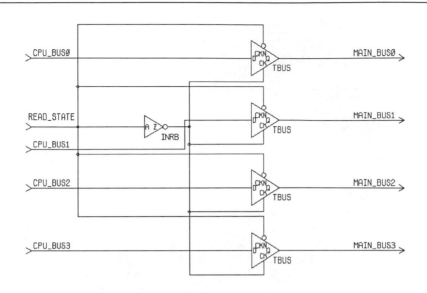

Figure 6-34 A bank of tri-state gates.

```
entity COUNT3_1S is
   port (DATA, CLOCK: in BIT;
         DETECT3_1S: out BIT);
end COUNT3_1S;

architecture SEQUENTIAL_BEHAVIOR of COUNT3_1S is
   type STATE is (COUNT0, COUNT1, COUNT2, COUNT3);
   signal CURRENT_STATE: STATE;
begin
   process
   begin
     wait until CLOCK = '0';

     case CURRENT_STATE is
       when COUNT0 =>
         DETECT3_1S <= '0';

         if DATA = '1' then
           CURRENT_STATE <= COUNT1;
         else                -- when DATA = '0'
           null;             -- CURRENT_STATE <= COUNT0;
         end if;
```

```
when COUNT1 =>
  if DATA = '1' then
    CURRENT_STATE <= COUNT2;
  else                  -- when DATA = 0
    CURRENT_STATE <= COUNT0;
  end if;
when COUNT2 =>
  if DATA = '1' then
    CURRENT_STATE <= COUNT3;
  else
    CURRENT_STATE <= COUNT0;
  end if;
when COUNT3 =>
  DETECT3_1S <= '1';

  if DATA = '0' then
    CURRENT_STATE <= COUNT0;
  end if;
end case;
end process;
end SEQUENTIAL_BEHAVIOR;
```

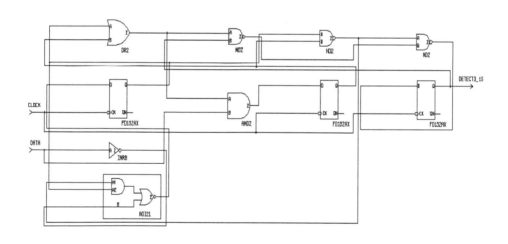

Figure 6-35 COUNT3_1S synthesized circuit.

Synthesis infers three flip-flops for this model, two for CURRENT_STATE and one for DETECT3_1S. See Figure 6-35. In the model, the output is latched since it is assigned a value under the control of a clock edge. If a latched output is not desired, then a second process statement has to be used in which the output DETECT3_1S is assigned a value. Such an architecture is shown in the following model.

```
architecture NO_LATCHED_OUPUT of COUNT3_1S is
   type STATE is (COUNT0, COUNT1, COUNT2, COUNT3);
   signal CURRENT_STATE: STATE;
begin
   -- This process only updates the next state (does not assign to outputs).
   UPDATE_STATE:
   process
   begin
      wait until CLOCK = '0';

      case CURRENT_STATE is
         when COUNT0 =>
            if DATA = '1' then
               CURRENT_STATE <= COUNT1;
            else                    -- when DATA = '0'
               null;                -- CURRENT_STATE <= COUNT0;
            end if;
         when COUNT1 =>
            if DATA = '1' then
               CURRENT_STATE <= COUNT2;
            else                    -- when DATA = 0
               CURRENT_STATE <= COUNT0;
            end if;
         when COUNT2 =>
            if DATA = '1' then
               CURRENT_STATE <= COUNT3;
            else
               CURRENT_STATE <= COUNT0;
            end if;
         when COUNT3 =>
            if DATA = '0' then
               CURRENT_STATE <= COUNT0;
            end if;
      end case;
   end process;

   -- This process computes the output based on the state information.
   ASSIGN_OUTPUT:
   process (CURRENT_STATE)
   begin
      case CURRENT_STATE is
         when COUNT0 =>
            DETECT3_1S <= '0';
         when COUNT1 | COUNT2 =>
```

```
        null;
    when COUNT3 =>
        DETECT3_1S <= '1';
    end case;
  end process;
end NO_LATCHED_OUTPUT;
```

In the architecture NO_LATCHED_OUTPUT, the output DETECT3_1S is not latched. Synthesis will therefore infer only two flip-flops (that models CURRENT_STATE).

6.23 A factorial model

Here is a model that generates the factorial of a number given in DATA. The result is output in FAC_OUT and EXP_OUT as mantissa and exponent respectively. The exponent is base 2. The signal RESET causes the model to reset.

```
library IEEE, SYNTH;
use IEEE.STD_LOGIC_1164.all;
use SYNTH.STD_LOGIC_ARITH.all;
entity FACEXP is
    port (RESET,                    -- Reset signal for calculation
          START,                    -- Start signal for calculation
          CLK: in STD_LOGIC;        -- Clock signal
          DATA: in UNSIGNED (4 downto 0); -- Input data
          DONE: out STD_LOGIC;      -- Acknowledge signal for operation
          FAC_OUT,                  -- Factorial
          EXP_OUT: out UNSIGNED (7 downto 0)); -- Exponent
end;

architecture FACEXP of FACEXP is
    signal STOP: STD_LOGIC;         -- Control signal for multiplication
    signal IN_LATCH: UNSIGNED (4 downto 0); -- Input register
    signal EXPONENT,                -- Exponent of result
           RESULT: UNSIGNED (7 downto 0); -- Output register
begin
    process
      variable RES_T, NXTRES_T, INL_T, NXTINL_T,
               EXP_T: INTEGER range 0 to 1024;
    begin
      wait until CLK = '1';
```

```
            if ((START = '1') and (STOP = '1')) or (RESET = '1') then
               RESULT <= "00000001";
               EXPONENT <= (others => '0');
               IN_LATCH <= DATA;
               STOP <= '0';
            else
               RES_T := TO_INTEGER (RESULT);
               EXP_T := TO_INTEGER (EXPONENT);
               INL_T := TO_INTEGER (IN_LATCH);

               if (INL_T > 1) and (STOP = '0') then
                  NXTRES_T := RES_T * INL_T;
                  NXTINL_T := INL_T - 1;
               else
                  NXTRES_T := RES_T;
                  NXTINL_T := INL_T;
               end if;

               if INL_T <= 1 then
                  STOP <= '1';
               end if;

               -- Normalization:
               for K in 1 to 5 loop
                  if NXTRES_T > 256 then
                     NXTRES_T := NXTRES_T / 2;
                     EXP_T := EXP_T + 1;
                  end if;
               end loop;

               RESULT <= TO_UNSIGNED (NXTRES_T, RESULT'LENGTH);
               EXPONENT <= TO_UNSIGNED(EXP_T, EXPONENT'LENGTH);
               IN_LATCH <= TO_UNSIGNED(NXTINL_T, IN_LATCH'LENGTH);
            end if;
         end process;

         DONE <= STOP;
         FAC_OUT <= RESULT;
         EXP_OUT <= EXPONENT;
      end FACEXP;
```

When synthesized, flip-flops are inferred for signals IN_LATCH, RESULT, EXPONENT and STOP.

6.24 A UART model

Here is a model of a complete UART circuit that can be synthesized. This circuit converts RS-232 serial input data into parallel data out, and the parallel input data into RS-232 serial data out. The data byte is 8 bits in length. There are four major blocks in this UART model, as shown in Figure 6-36: RX, the receiver block, TX, the transmitter block, DIV, the clock divider and MP, the microprocessor block.

The first block DIV is a frequency divider. This block has 2 modes of operation, the normal mode and the test mode. In the test mode, the UART chip runs 16 times faster than in the normal mode. Also, the transmission data rate of the UART chip is 16 times faster than the receiving rate. Each block is initialized by setting the reset line low by applying a '0' to port MR. The TX block accepts 8-bit parallel data from the microprocessor interface (MP) block and transmits it serially to the RS-232 port through port DOUT. Conversely, the RX block receives serial data input, and sends it in 8-bit parallel format to the MP block. Again, the transmitter runs at 16 times the speed of the receiver. The microprocessor interface (MP) block asynchronously controls the parallel data flow between the RX/TX blocks and the microprocessor data bus.

The UART top-level model glues all these blocks together using component instantiations. The microprocessor entity, MP, is described in the structural style, that is, using components. The remaining three are described using the behavioral style.

The UART top-level model follows.

```
library IEEE, SYNTH;
use IEEE.STD_LOGIC_1164.all;
use SYNTH.GENERIC_COMP.all; -- Include component declarations.
entity UART is
    port (DIN, CLK, MR, AS, WRN, RDN, CSN, TEST: in STD_ULOGIC;
          UDIN: in STD_ULOGIC_VECTOR(0 to 7);
          INTQN, DOUT: out STD_ULOGIC;
          UDOUT: out STD_ULOGIC_VECTOR(0 to 7));
end UART;

architecture TOP_LEVEL of UART is
    -- The major building blocks:
    component DIV
        port (CK, RESET, TSN: in STD_ULOGIC;
              ENA: out STD_ULOGIC);
```

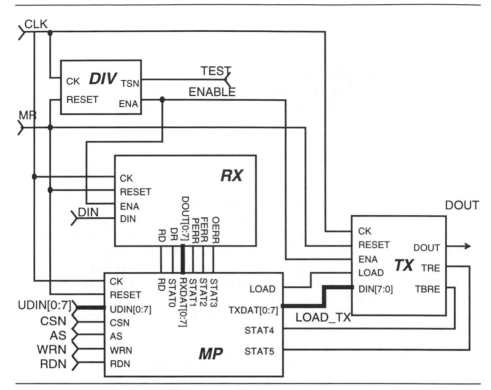

Figure 6-36 The UART circuit.

```
        end component;
        component RX
            port (CK, RESET, ENA, DIN, RD: in STD_ULOGIC;
                DOUTO: out STD_ULOGIC_VECTOR(0 to 7);
                DRO, PERRO, FERRO, OERRO: out STD_ULOGIC);
        end component;
        component TX
            port (CK, RESET, ENABLE, TLOAD: in STD_ULOGIC;
                DIN: in STD_ULOGIC_VECTOR(0 to 7);
                DOUT, TRE, TBRE: out STD_ULOGIC);
        end component;
        component MP
            port (CK, RESET, CSN, AS, WRN, RDN: in STD_ULOGIC;
                UDIN, RXDAT: in STD_ULOGIC_VECTOR(0 to 7);
                STAT: in STD_ULOGIC_VECTOR(0 to 5);
                LOADVE: inout STD_ULOGIC;
                TXDAT: out STD_ULOGIC_VECTOR(0 to 7);
                RD: inout STD_ULOGIC;
                INTQN: out STD_ULOGIC;
```

```
                    UDOUT: out STD_ULOGIC_VECTOR (0 to 7));
          end component;

          for all: DIV use entity WORK.DIV(DIV_BEH);
          for all: RX use entity WORK.RX(RX_BEH);
          for all: TX use entity WORK.TX(TX_BEH);
          for all: MP use entity WORK.MP;
          for all: BUF use entity SYNTH.BUF;
          for all: INRB use entity SYNTH.INRB;

          signal CKI, LINE_IN, MRIN, TESTBUF, T_DOUT, CK, RESET,
              TESTN, ENABLE, CKIN, MRINN, RX_READY, R_PERR, R_FERR,
              R_OERR, T_TBRE, TX_BUSYN, LOAD_TX,
              READ_RX: STD_ULOGIC;
          signal R_DOUT, M_TXDAT: STD_ULOGIC_VECTOR(0 to 7);
          signal STAT: STD_ULOGIC_VECTOR(0 to 5);
      begin
        LCLKBUF: BUF port map (CLK, CKI);
        LDINBUF: BUF port map (DIN, LINE_IN);
        LMRBUF: BUF port map (MR, MRIN);
        LTESTBUF: BUF port map (TEST, TESTBUF);
        LDOUT: BUF port map (T_DOUT, DOUT);
        LD: DIV port map (CK, RESET, TESTN, ENABLE);
        LCK: INRB port map (CKIN, CK);
        LRESET: INRB port map (MRINN, RESET);
        LCKG1: INRB port map (CKI, CKIN);
        LMRG1: INRB port map (MRIN, MRINN);
        LTESTN: INRB port map (TESTBUF, TESTN);
        LM: MP port map (CK => CK, RESET => RESET, CSN => CSN,
            AS => AS, WRN => WRN, RDN => RDN, UDIN => UDIN,
            RXDAT => R_DOUT, STAT(0) => RX_READY, STAT(1) => R_PERR,
            STAT(2) => R_FERR, STAT(3) => R_OERR, STAT(4) => T_TBRE,
            STAT(5) => TX_BUSYN, LOADVE => LOAD_TX,
            TXDAT => M_TXDAT, RD => READ_RX, INTQN => INTQN,
            UDOUT => UDOUT);
        LR: RX port map (CK, RESET, ENABLE, LINE_IN, READ_RX,
            R_DOUT, RX_READY, R_PERR, R_FERR, R_OERR);
        LT: TX port map (CK, RESET, ENABLE, LOAD_TX,
            M_TXDAT, T_DOUT, TX_BUSYN, T_TBRE);
      end TOP_LEVEL;
```

The microprocessor block MP is described next. This is a block described entirely using components, that is, it is described at the structural level.

```vhdl
library IEEE;
use IEEE.STD_LOGIC_1164.all;
entity MP is
   port (CK, RESET, CSN, AS, WRN, RDN: in STD_ULOGIC;
         UDIN, RXDAT: in STD_ULOGIC_VECTOR (0 to 7);
         STAT: in STD_ULOGIC_VECTOR (0 to 5);
         LOADVE: inout STD_ULOGIC;
         TXDAT: out STD_ULOGIC_VECTOR (0 to 7);
         RD: inout STD_ULOGIC;
         INTQN: out STD_ULOGIC;
         UDOUT: out STD_ULOGIC_VECTOR (0 to 7));
end MP;

library SYNTH;
use SYNTH.GENERIC_COMP.all;
architecture MP_STR of MP is
   for all: AND2 use entity SYNTH.AND2;
   for all: BN20T20D use entity SYNTH.BN20T20D;
   for all: FD1P3AX use entity SYNTH.FD1P3AX;
   for all: FD1S1A use entity SYNTH.FD1S1A;
   for all: FD1S3EX use entity SYNTH.FD1S3EX;
   for all: FS0S1D use entity SYNTH.FS0S1D;
   for all: INRB use entity SYNTH.INRB;
   for all: ND2 use entity SYNTH.ND2;
   for all: NR2 use entity SYNTH.NR2;
   for all: NR3 use entity SYNTH.NR3;
   for all: XOR2Z use entity SYNTH.XOR2Z;
   for all: BUF use entity SYNTH.BUF;
   for all: OR2 use entity SYNTH.OR2;
   for all: AOI22 use entity SYNTH.AOI22;

   signal QB_Q, QA_QN, ENAFFO, QA_Q, RESLOG, WRT, ENA42,
          SETLOG, ENA40, RDT, STADRI, ASBUF, CSBUF, RDBUF, WRBUF,
          RDTE, XOLD_Z, UC_LOAD_QN, PRELOAD_Q,
          UC_PRELOAD_QN, LOG_Q, UC_QB_QN, RESETN, UC_LOG_QN,
          UC_XOLD_Z1, QC, QD, RDSYNFB, ENA41, RDTLOG, RXDRI,
          INTN, ORINT, UC_INTFF_Q, RDSYN, UC_QC_QN, UC_QD_QN,
          XORD_Z, UC_QE_QN, UC_RDSYN_QN, UC_XORD_Z1
           : STD_ULOGIC;
   signal BUSOUT, INVOUT, DATIN, UPD_Q, RXG, UC_UPD_QN,
          UC_A_QN, A, UC_DAT_QN: STD_ULOGIC_VECTOR (0 to 7);
   signal SG: STD_ULOGIC_VECTOR(0 to 5);
   signal DEC: STD_ULOGIC_VECTOR (0 to 9);
begin
   LENAFFO: AND2 port map (QB_Q, QA_QN, ENAFFO);
   LRESLOG: AND2 port map (QB_Q, QA_Q, RESLOG);
   LSETLOG: AND2 port map (WRT, ENA42, SETLOG);
```

LSTADRI: AND2 **port map** (ENA40, RDT, STADRI);
LASBUF: BUF **port map** (AS, ASBUF);
LCSBUF: BUF **port map** (CSN, CSBUF);
LRDBUF: BUF **port map** (RDN, RDBUF);
LWRBUF: BUF **port map** (WRN, WRBUF);

G0: **for** J **in** 0 **to** 7 **generate**
    LADBUF: BN20T20D **port map** (BUSOUT(J), RDTE, INVOUT(J),
            UDIN(J), DATIN(7-J), UDOUT(J));
    LDAT: FD1P3AX **port map** (UPD_Q(J), ENAFFO, CK,
            TXDAT(J), UC_DAT_QN(J));
    LA: FD1S1A **port map** (DATIN(7-J), ASBUF, A(J), UC_A_QN(J));
    LUPD: FD1S1A **port map** (DATIN(7-J), WRT, UPD_Q(J),
            UC_UPD_QN(J));
    LINVOUT: INRB **port map** (RDTE, INVOUT(J));
LRXG: INRB **port map** (RXDAT(J), RXG(J));
end generate G0;

LLOAD: FD1S3EX **port map** (XOLD_Z, CK, RESET, LOADVE,
        UC_LOAD_QN);
LPRELOAD: FD1S3EX **port map** (QB_Q, CK, RESET, PRELOAD_Q,
        UC_PRELOAD_QN);
LQA: FD1S3EX **port map** (LOG_Q, CK, RESET, QA_Q, QA_QN);
LQB: FD1S3EX **port map** (QA_Q, CK, RESET, QB_Q, UC_QB_QN);
LLOG: FS0S1D **port map** (SETLOG, RESLOG, RESETN,
        LOG_Q, UC_LOG_QN);
LDEC3: INRB **port map** (DEC(1), DEC(3));
LDEC4: ND2 **port map** (DEC(1), A(1), DEC(4));
LDEC5: ND2 **port map** (DEC(2), A(6), DEC(5));
LDEC7: NR2 **port map** (DEC(4), DEC(5), ENA42);
LWRT: NR2 **port map** (CSBUF, WRBUF, WRT);
LRDT1: NR2 **port map** (CSBUF, RDBUF, RDT);
LRDT2: NR2 **port map** (CSBUF, RDBUF, RDTE);
LDEC1: NR3 **port map** (A(0), A(2), A(3), DEC(1));
LDEC2: NR3 **port map** (A(4), A(5), A(7), DEC(2));
LDEC6: NR3 **port map** (DEC(5), DEC(3), A(1), ENA40);
LXOLD: XOR2Z **port map** (LOADVE, PRELOAD_Q, XOLD_Z,
        UC_XOLD_Z1);
LRDSUNFB: AND2 **port map** (QC, QD, RDSYNFB);
LRDTLOG: AND2 **port map** (RDT, ENA41, RDTLOG);
LRXDRI: AND2 **port map** (ENA41, RDT, RXDRI);
LINTQ: BUF **port map** (INTN, INTQN);
LINTFF: FD1S3EX **port map** (ORINT, CK, RESET, UC_INTFF_Q, INTN);
LQC: FD1S3EX **port map** (RDSYN, CK, RESET, QC, UC_QC_QN);
LQD: FD1S3EX **port map** (QC, CK, RESET, QD, UC_QD_QN);
LQE: FD1S3EX **port map** (XORD_Z, CK, RESET, RD, UC_QE_QN);
LRDSYN: FS0S1D **port map** (RDTLOG, RDSYNFB, RESETN,

```
                    RDSYN, UC_RDSYN_QN);
        LRESETN: INRB port map (RESET, RESETN);

        G1: for J in 0 to 5 generate
          LSG: INRB port map (STAT(J), SG(J));
          LMUX: AOI22 port map (RXG(J), RXDRI, SG(J), STADRI,
                  BUSOUT(J));
        end generate G1;

        LDEC9: ND2 port map (DEC(8), A(0), DEC(9));
        LDEC10: NR2 port map (DEC(5), DEC(9), ENA41);
        LDEC8: NR3 port map (A(1), A(2), A(3), DEC(8));
        LORINT: OR2 port map (STAT(0), STAT(4), ORINT);
        LMUX6: ND2 port map (RXG(6), RXDRI, BUSOUT(6));
        LMUX7: ND2 port map (RXG(7), RXDRI, BUSOUT(7));
        LXORD: XOR2Z port map (RD, QD, XORD_Z, UC_XORD_Z1);
      end MP_STR;
```

Here is the behavioral model for the transmitter block TX. This model is a synthesizable model. Rising-edge-triggered flip-flops are inferred for signals TBR, TR, STRE, STBRE, DOUT, CBIT and PA; this is because these signals are assigned values under the control of clock CK.

```
        library IEEE, SYNTH;
        use IEEE.STD_LOGIC_1164.all;
        use SYNTH.STD_LOGIC_ARITH.all;
        entity TX is
          port (CK, RESET, ENABLE, TLOAD: in STD_LOGIC;
                DIN: in STD_LOGIC_VECTOR(7 downto 0);
                DOUT,
                TRE,    -- Tx reg empty.
                TBRE    -- Tx buf empty.
                  : out STD_LOGIC);
        end TX;

        architecture TX_BEH of TX is
          signal TBR, TR: STD_LOGIC_VECTOR(7 downto 0);
          signal CBIT: UNSIGNED(3 downto 0);
          signal PA: STD_LOGIC;
          signal STBRE: STD_LOGIC;
          signal STRE: STD_LOGIC;
        begin
          process (CK, RESET, ENABLE, TLOAD, DIN, TBR, TR, CBIT,
                    PA, STBRE, STRE)
            variable TEMP_TRE: STD_LOGIC;
            constant CONE: UNSIGNED(3 downto 0) := "0001";
```

```
begin
  if RISING_EDGE(CK) then
    if RESET = '0' then
      STRE <= '1';
      STBRE <= '1';
      DOUT <= '1';
      CBIT <= "0000";
      PA <= '0';
    else
      if TLOAD = '1' then
        TBR <= DIN;
        STBRE <= '0';
      else
        if ENABLE = '1' then
          if (STBRE = '0') and (STRE = '1') then
            TR <= TBR;
            STRE <= '0';
            TEMP_TRE := '0';
            STBRE <= '1';
          else
            TEMP_TRE := STRE;
          end if;

          if TEMP_TRE = '0' then
            case CBIT is
              when "0000" =>
                DOUT <= '0';
                CBIT <= CBIT + CONE;
              when "0001" | "0010" | "0011" |
                   "0100" | "0101" | "0110" |
                   "0111" | "1000" =>
                DOUT <= TR(0);
                PA <= PA xor TR(0);
                TR <= '1' & TR(7 downto 1);
                CBIT <= CBIT + CONE;

              when "1001" =>
                DOUT <= PA;
                PA <= '0';
                TR <= '1' & TR(7 downto 1);
                CBIT <= CBIT + CONE;
              when "1010" =>
                DOUT <= TR(0);
                TR <= '1' & TR(7 downto 1);
                CBIT <= CBIT + CONE;
              when "1011" =>
                DOUT <= TR(0);
```

```
                        STRE <= '1';
                        TR <= '1' & TR(7 downto 1);
                        CBIT <= "0000";
                    when others =>
                        null;
                end case;
              end if;
            end if;
          end if;
        end if;
      end if;

      TRE <= STRE;
      TBRE <= STBRE;
    end process;
  end TX_BEH;
```

Here is the behavioral model for the receiver block RX. This model is also synthesizable. Flip-flops are inferred for signals START, CBIT, CSAM, DI, PI, SR, DR, DOUT, PERR, FERR and OERR.

```
library IEEE, SYNTH;
use IEEE.STD_LOGIC_1164.all;
use SYNTH.STD_LOGIC_ARITH.all;
entity RX is
  port (CK, RESET, ENA, DIN, RD: in STD_ULOGIC;
        DOUTO: out STD_ULOGIC_VECTOR (7 downto 0);
        DRO, PERRO, FERRO, OERRO: out STD_ULOGIC);
end RX;

architecture RX_BEH of RX is
  signal START: STD_ULOGIC;
  signal CBIT, CSAM: UNSIGNED(3 downto 0);
  signal DI, PI: STD_ULOGIC;
  signal SR: STD_ULOGIC_VECTOR (7 downto 0);
  signal DR: STD_ULOGIC;
  signal DOUT: STD_ULOGIC_VECTOR(7 downto 0);
  signal PERR, FERR, OERR: STD_ULOGIC;
begin
  process (CK, RESET, ENA, DIN, RD, START, CBIT, CSAM,
           DI, PI, SR, DR, DOUT, PERR, FERR, OERR)
    variable TCBIT, TCSAM: INTEGER range 0 to 15;
    constant CONE: UNSIGNED(3 downto 0) := "0001";
  begin
    if RISING_EDGE(CK) then
      TCBIT := TO_INTEGER (CBIT);
      TCSAM := TO_INTEGER (CSAM);
```

```
if RESET = '0' then        -- Reset.
  CBIT <= "0000";
  CSAM <= "0000";
  START <= '0';
  PI <= '0';
  DR <= '0';
  PERR <= '0';
  FERR <= '0';
  OERR <= '0';
else
  if RD = '1' then
    DR <= '0';
  end if;

  if ENA = '1' then
    if START = '0' then
      if DIN = '0' then
        CSAM <= CSAM + CONE;
        START <= '1';
      end if;
    else
      if TCSAM = 8 then
        DI <= DIN;
        CSAM <= CSAM + CONE;
      else
        if TCSAM = 15 then
          case TCBIT is
            when 0 =>
              if DI = '1' then
                START <= '0';
              else
                CBIT <= CBIT + CONE;
              end if;
              CSAM <= CSAM + CONE;
            when 1 | 2 | 3 | 4 | 5 | 6 | 7 | 8 =>
              CBIT <= CBIT + CONE;
              CSAM <= CSAM + CONE;
              PI <= PI xor DI;
              SR <= DI & SR(7 downto 1);
            when 9 =>
              CBIT <= CBIT + CONE;
              CSAM <= CSAM + CONE;
              PI <= PI xor DI;
            when 10 =>
              PERR <= PI;
              PI <= '0';
```

```
                             if DI = '0' then
                                FERR <= '1';
                             else
                                FERR <= '0';
                             end if;

                             if DR = '1' then
                                OERR <= '1';
                             else
                                OERR <= '0';
                             end if;

                             DR <= '1';
                             DOUT <= SR;
                             CBIT <= "0000";
                             START <= '0';
                          when others =>
                             null;
                        end case;
                     else
                        CSAM <= CSAM + CONE;
                     end if;
                  end if;
               end if;
            end if;
         end if;
      end if;

      DRO <= DR;
      DOUTO <= DOUT;
      PERRO <= PERR;
      FERRO <= FERR;
      OERRO <= OERR;
   end process;
end RX_BEH;
```

Here is a synthesizable model for the divider block DIV. This circuit produces a pulse every sixteen clock cycles. If signal TESTN is '0', it operates
in the fast mode, that is, a pulse is produced for every clock cycle. Signal
COUNTER is inferred as flip-flops.

```
library IEEE, SYNTH;
use IEEE.STD_LOGIC_1164.all;
use SYNTH.STD_LOGIC_ARITH.all;
entity DIV is
   port (CK, RESET, TESTN: in STD_ULOGIC;
```

```
                    ENA: out STD_ULOGIC);
          end DIV;

          architecture DIV_BEH of DIV is
            signal COUNTER: UNSIGNED(3 downto 0);
          begin
            process (CK, RESET, TESTN, COUNTER)
              constant CONE: UNSIGNED(3 downto 0) := "0001";
            begin
              -- Synchronous section:
              if RISING_EDGE(CK) then
                if RESET = '0' then
                  COUNTER <= "0000";
                else
                  if TESTN = '0' then
                    COUNTER <= "1111";
                  else
                    COUNTER <= COUNTER + CONE;
                  end if;
                end if;
              end if;

              -- Combinational section:
              if COUNTER = "1111" then
                ENA <= '1';
              else
                ENA <= '0';
              end if;
            end process;
          end DIV_BEH;
```

6.25 A blackjack model

Here is a synthesizable model of a blackjack program. This program is played with a deck of cards. Cards 2 to 10 have values equal to their face value, and an ace has a value of either 1 or 11. The object of the game is to accept a number of random cards such that the total score (sum of values of all cards) is as close as possible to 21 without exceeding 21.

When a new card is inserted, signal CARD_RDY is true, and signal CARD_VALUE has the value of the card. The signal REQUEST_CARD indicates when the program is ready to accept a new card. If a sequence of cards is accepted such that the total falls between 17 and 21, then signal WON is set to true, indicating that the game has been won. If total exceeds 21, then the program checks to see if an ace was accepted as a 1 or a 10; if it was accepted as a 10, the value of ace is changed to 1 and the program gets ready to accept a new card; if not, signal LOST is set to true indicating that it has lost. The state sequencing is controlled by the signal CLOCK. This model is a classic example of a Moore finite state machine.

```
entity BLACKJACK is
   port (CARD_RDY: in BOOLEAN;
         CARD_VALUE: in INTEGER;
         INSERT_CARD, WON, LOST: out BOOLEAN;
         CLOCK: in BIT);
end BLACKJACK;

architecture STATE_MACHINE of BLACKJACK is
   type STATE_TYPE is (INITIAL_ST, GETCARD_ST, REMCARD_ST,
            ADD_ST, CHECK_ST, WIN_ST, BACKUP_ST, LOSE_ST);
   signal BJ_STATE: STATE_TYPE;
begin
  process
    variable CURRENT_CARD_VALUE, TOTAL: NATURAL;
    variable ACE_AS_11: BOOLEAN;
  begin
    wait until CLOCK = '0';

    case BJ_STATE is
      when INITIAL_ST =>
        TOTAL := 0;
        ACE_AS_11 := FALSE;
        WON <= FALSE;
        LOST <= FALSE;
        BJ_STATE <= GETCARD_ST;

      when GETCARD_ST =>
        INSERT_CARD <= TRUE;

        if CARD_RDY then
          CURRENT_CARD_VALUE := CARD_VALUE;
          BJ_STATE <= REMCARD_ST;
        end if;

      when REMCARD_ST =>
        if CARD_RDY then
          BJ_STATE <= REMCARD_ST;
          INSERT_CARD <= FALSE;
        else
          BJ_STATE <= ADD_ST;
```

```
      end if;

when ADD_ST =>
  if (not ACE_AS_11) and
      (CURRENT_CARD_VALUE = 1) then
    CURRENT_CARD_VALUE := 10;
    ACE_AS_11 := TRUE;
  end if;

  TOTAL := TOTAL + CURRENT_CARD_VALUE;
  BJ_STATE <= CHECK_ST;

when CHECK_ST =>
  if TOTAL < 17 then
    BJ_STATE <= GETCARD_ST;
  elsif TOTAL < 22 then
    BJ_STATE <= WIN_ST;
  else
    BJ_STATE <= BACKUP_ST;
  end if;

when BACKUP_ST =>
  if ACE_AS_11 then
    TOTAL := TOTAL - 10;
    ACE_AS_11 := FALSE;
    BJ_STATE <= CHECK_ST;
  else
    BJ_STATE <= LOSE_ST;
  end if;

when LOSE_ST =>
  LOST <= TRUE;
  INSERT_CARD <= TRUE;


  if CARD_RDY then
    BJ_STATE <= INITIAL_ST;
  end if;

when WIN_ST =>
  WON <= TRUE;
  INSERT_CARD <= TRUE;

  if CARD_RDY then
    BJ_STATE <= INITIAL_ST;
  end if;
```

```
        end case;
      end process;
    end STATE_MACHINE;
```

❑

Appendix A

Synthesizable
Constructs

To give an idea of what VHDL constructs are synthesizable, this appendix gives a listing of the synthesizable VHDL constructs that are recognized by the ArchSyn synthesis system, v14.0. The material is organized to reflect the contents of the IEEE Standard VHDL Language Reference Manual, IEEE Std 1076-1993.

Constructs that have relevance only to simulation are identified as "ignored constructs" and constructs that are not synthesizable are marked as "not synthesizable". The constructs are categorized as follows:

   i.   *Supported*: Constructs that get synthesized into hardware.
   ii. *Not supported*: Synthesis terminates when such a construct is present in the input file.

iii. *Ignored*: Warning messages are issued during synthesis, except for declarations and specifications.

In the following tables, the first column mentions the VHDL feature, the second column indicates whether the feature is supported or not, and the third column is for comments and exceptions.

Design Entities and Configurations

Entity Declarations		
Entity Header	Supported	Generics are also supported. Default values for ports are ignored.
Entity Declarative Part	Supported	
Entity Statements	Ignored	
Architecture Bodies	Supported	Multiple architecture bodies are allowed.
Configurations	Ignored	

Subprograms and Packages

Subprogram Declarations	Supported	Recursion is not supported. Default values for formal parameters not supported.
Subprogram Bodies	Supported	
Subprogram Overloading	Supported	
Operator Overloading	Supported	
Resolution Functions	Ignored	Signals are connected together, based on a global option specified: *wired-and*: drivers are and'ed together. *wired-or*: drivers are or'ed together. *tri-state*: drivers connected to each other.
Package Declarations	Supported	
Package Bodies	Supported	

Types

Scalar Types		
Enumeration Types	Supported	Null ranges are not supported.
Integer Types	Supported	Null ranges are not supported. Integers allowed in range $-(2^{31} - 1)$ to $+(2^{31} - 1)$.

Types

Physical Types	Ignored	Use of physical types are not supported. Physical type literals are ignored.
Floating Point Types	Ignored	Use of floating point types and literals are not supported.
Composite Types		
Array Types	Supported	More than two dimension not supported. Null arrays are not supported.
Record Types	Supported	
Access Types	Ignored	Use of access types is not supported.
File Types	Ignored	Use of file types is not supported.
Incomplete Type Declarations	Ignored	

Declarations

Type Declarations	Supported	
Subtype declarations	Supported	
Object Declarations		
Constant Declarations	Supported	

Declarations

Signal Declarations	Supported	Register and bus declarations are not supported. Resolution functions are ignored. Initial values are ignored.
Variable Declarations	Supported	Initial values are ignored.
File Declarations	Ignored	
Interface Declarations	Supported	Linkage mode is not supported.
Alias Declarations	Ignored	
Attribute Declarations	Supported	
Component Declarations	Supported	

Specifications

Attribute Specifications	Supported	
Configuration Specifications	Ignored	
Disconnection Specifications	Ignored	

Names

Simple Names	Supported	
Selected Names	Supported	
Indexed Names	Supported	
Slice Names	Supported	Null slices are not supported.
Attribute Names		
Predefined array attributes	Supported	The supported ones are: 'BASE, 'LEFT, 'RIGHT, 'HIGH, 'LOW, 'RANGE, 'REVERSE_RANGE, 'LENGTH, 'EVENT, and 'STABLE. Attributes 'EVENT and 'STABLE are supported only in wait and if statements to specify events on clocks.
User-defined attributes	Supported	The attribute ENUM_TYPE_ENCODING is the only one supported.

Expressions

Operators		
Logical operators	Supported	
Relational operators	Supported	
Adding operators	Supported	
Multiplying operators	Supported	mod and rem supported only for positive numbers.

Expressions

Miscellaneous operators	Supported	Exponentiation supported only if both operands are constants or if left operand is a power of two.
Operands		
Integer literals	Supported	
Floating point literals	Not supported	
Based literals	Supported	
Physical literals	Ignored	
Enumeration literals	Supported	
String literals	Supported	Only under the condition that each character has a single bit encoded value.
Bit-string literals	Supported	
Null literals	Not supported	
Aggregates	Supported	
Function Calls	Supported	
Qualified Expressions	Supported	
Type Conversions	Supported	
Allocators	Not supported	
Static Expressions	Supported	
Universal Expressions	Supported	

Sequential Statements

Wait Statement	Supported	Only the **"wait until"** form is supported and it can only be used to specify clock-related events. The `wait` statement has the form: **wait until** *clock_expression* ; The `wait` statement, if present, must be the first statement in a process.
Assertion Statement	Ignored	
Signal Assignment Statement	Supported	`guarded` option not supported. `transport` option is ignored. `after` clause is ignored. Multiple waveform elements are not supported.
Variable Assignment Statement	Supported	
Procedure call Statement	Supported	Type conversion on formal parameters is not supported.
If Statement	Supported	
Case Statement	Supported	
Loop Statement		
For-iteration scheme	Supported	Ranges must be globally static.
While-iteration scheme	Not supported	
No-iteration scheme	Not supported	
Next Statement	Supported	

Sequential Statements

Exit Statement	Supported	
Return Statement	Supported	
Null Statement	Supported	

Concurrent Statements

Block Statement	Supported	Guards are not supported. Ports and generics are not supported.
Process Statement	Supported	Sensitivity list is ignored.
Concurrent Procedure call	Supported	
Concurrent Assertion Statement	Ignored	
Concurrent Signal Assignment Statement	Supported	guarded option not supported. transport option is ignored. after clause is ignored. Multiple waveform elements are not supported. unaffected not supported.
Conditional Signal Assignment	Supported	
Selected Signal Assignment	Supported	
Component Instantiation Statement	Supported	Type conversion on a formal port is not supported.
Generate Statement	Supported	

Design Units and Analysis

Design Units	Supported	Separate compilation allowed.
Design Libraries	Supported	
Context Clauses	Supported	

Pre-defined Language Environment

Predefined Attributes	Supported	The only supported ones are: 'BASE, 'LEFT, 'RIGHT, 'HIGH, 'LOW, 'RANGE, 'REVERSE_RANGE, 'LENGTH, 'EVENT, and 'STABLE. Attributes 'EVENT and 'STABLE are supported only in wait and if statements to specify events on clocks.
STANDARD package	Supported	Type STRING is not supported. Type TIME is ignored. Function NOW is ignored.
TEXTIO package	Not supported	

❑

Appendix B

An Arithmetic Package

This appendix contains an arithmetic package based on the IEEE standard STD_LOGIC_1164 package. Many examples in this text use this package.

Package STD_LOGIC_ARITH

This package defines two array types UNSIGNED and SIGNED of element type STD_LOGIC. The type SIGNED represents a signed number in two's complement form, while the type UNSIGNED represents unsigned numbers. The package also contains overloaded operator functions that operate on these types. Conversion functions are also defined in this package.

```
-- This package resides in library SYNTH.
library IEEE;
use IEEE.STD_LOGIC_1164.all;
package STD_LOGIC_ARITH is
   -- The types UNSIGNED and SIGNED:
   type UNSIGNED is array (NATURAL range <>) of STD_LOGIC;
   type SIGNED is array (NATURAL range <>) of STD_LOGIC;

   -- Conversion functions:
   function TO_INTEGER (U: UNSIGNED) return INTEGER;
   function TO_INTEGER (S: SIGNED) return INTEGER;

   function TO_STDLOGICVECTOR (U: UNSIGNED;
              SIZE : INTEGER) return STD_LOGIC_VECTOR;
   subtype LONG is STD_LOGIC_VECTOR (31 downto 0);
   function TO_STDLOGICVECTOR (I : INTEGER) return LONG;
   function TO_STDLOGICVECTOR (I, SIZE : INTEGER)
              return STD_LOGIC_VECTOR;

   function TO_UNSIGNED (I, SIZE : INTEGER) return UNSIGNED;
   function TO_UNSIGNED (S: SIGNED; SIZE: INTEGER)
              return UNSIGNED;
   function TO_UNSIGNED (U: UNSIGNED; SIZE: INTEGER)
              return UNSIGNED;

   function TO_SIGNED (I, SIZE : INTEGER) return SIGNED;
   function TO_SIGNED (U : UNSIGNED; SIZE : INTEGER)
              return SIGNED;
   function TO_SIGNED (S: SIGNED; SIZE: INTEGER) return SIGNED;

   function TO_STDULOGIC (C: CHARACTER) return STD_ULOGIC;
   function TO_CHARACTER (S: STD_ULOGIC) return CHARACTER;

   -- Binary arithmetic functions:
   function "+" (L: UNSIGNED; R: UNSIGNED) return UNSIGNED;
   function "+" (L: SIGNED; R: SIGNED) return SIGNED;
   function "+" (L: SIGNED; R: INTEGER) return SIGNED;
   function "+" (L: INTEGER; R: SIGNED) return SIGNED;
   function "+" (L: UNSIGNED; R: INTEGER) return UNSIGNED;
   function "+" (L: INTEGER; R: UNSIGNED) return UNSIGNED;

   function "-" (L: UNSIGNED; R: UNSIGNED) return UNSIGNED;
   function "-" (L: SIGNED; R: SIGNED) return SIGNED;
   function "-" (L: SIGNED; R: INTEGER) return SIGNED;
   function "-" (L: INTEGER; R: SIGNED) return SIGNED;
   function "-" (L: UNSIGNED; R: INTEGER) return UNSIGNED;
   function "-" (L: INTEGER; R: UNSIGNED) return UNSIGNED;
```

```
function "*" (L: UNSIGNED; R: UNSIGNED) return UNSIGNED;
function "*" (L: SIGNED; R: SIGNED) return SIGNED;

function "/" (L: UNSIGNED; R: UNSIGNED) return UNSIGNED;
function "/" (L: SIGNED; R: SIGNED) return SIGNED;

function "mod" (L: UNSIGNED; R: UNSIGNED) return UNSIGNED;
function "mod" (L: SIGNED; R: SIGNED) return SIGNED;

function "rem" (L: UNSIGNED; R: UNSIGNED) return UNSIGNED;
function "rem" (L: SIGNED; R: SIGNED) return SIGNED;

-- Unary arithmetic functions:
function "-" (L: SIGNED) return SIGNED;
function "abs" (L: SIGNED) return SIGNED;

-- Comparison functions:
function "<" (L: UNSIGNED; R: UNSIGNED) return BOOLEAN;
function "<" (L: UNSIGNED; R: INTEGER) return BOOLEAN;
function "<" (L: INTEGER; R: UNSIGNED) return BOOLEAN;
function "<" (L: INTEGER; R: SIGNED) return BOOLEAN;
function "<" (L: SIGNED; R: SIGNED) return BOOLEAN;
function "<" (L: SIGNED; R: INTEGER) return BOOLEAN;

function "<=" (L: UNSIGNED; R: UNSIGNED) return BOOLEAN;
function "<=" (L: UNSIGNED; R: INTEGER) return BOOLEAN;
function "<=" (L: INTEGER; R: UNSIGNED) return BOOLEAN;
function "<=" (L: INTEGER; R: SIGNED) return BOOLEAN;
function "<=" (L: SIGNED; R: SIGNED) return BOOLEAN;
function "<=" (L: SIGNED; R: INTEGER) return BOOLEAN;

function ">=" (L: UNSIGNED; R: UNSIGNED) return BOOLEAN;
function ">=" (L: UNSIGNED; R: INTEGER) return BOOLEAN;
function ">=" (L: INTEGER; R: UNSIGNED) return BOOLEAN;
function ">=" (L: INTEGER; R: SIGNED) return BOOLEAN;
function ">=" (L: SIGNED; R: SIGNED) return BOOLEAN;
function ">=" (L: SIGNED; R: INTEGER) return BOOLEAN;

function ">" (L: UNSIGNED; R: UNSIGNED) return BOOLEAN;
function ">" (L: UNSIGNED; R: INTEGER) return BOOLEAN;
function ">" (L: INTEGER; R: UNSIGNED) return BOOLEAN;
function ">" (L: INTEGER; R: SIGNED) return BOOLEAN;
function ">" (L: SIGNED; R: SIGNED) return BOOLEAN;
function ">" (L: SIGNED; R: INTEGER) return BOOLEAN;
```

```
function "=" (L: UNSIGNED; R: UNSIGNED) return BOOLEAN;
function "=" (L: UNSIGNED; R: INTEGER) return BOOLEAN;
function "=" (L: INTEGER; R: UNSIGNED) return BOOLEAN;
function "=" (L: INTEGER; R: SIGNED) return BOOLEAN;
function "=" (L: SIGNED; R: SIGNED) return BOOLEAN;
function "=" (L: SIGNED; R: INTEGER) return BOOLEAN;

function "/=" (L: UNSIGNED; R: UNSIGNED) return BOOLEAN;
function "/=" (L: UNSIGNED; R: INTEGER) return BOOLEAN;
function "/=" (L: INTEGER; R: UNSIGNED) return BOOLEAN;
function "/=" (L: INTEGER; R: SIGNED) return BOOLEAN;
function "/=" (L: SIGNED; R: SIGNED) return BOOLEAN;
function "/=" (L: SIGNED; R: INTEGER) return BOOLEAN;

-- Logical operations:
function "and" (L, R: UNSIGNED) return UNSIGNED;
function "nand" (L, R: UNSIGNED) return UNSIGNED;
function "or" (L, R: UNSIGNED) return UNSIGNED;
function "nor" (L, R: UNSIGNED) return UNSIGNED;
function "xor" (L, R: UNSIGNED) return UNSIGNED;
function "not" (L: UNSIGNED) return UNSIGNED;

function "and" (L, R: SIGNED) return SIGNED;
function "nand" (L, R: SIGNED) return SIGNED;
function "or" (L, R: SIGNED) return SIGNED;
function "nor" (L, R: SIGNED) return SIGNED;
function "xor" (L, R: SIGNED) return SIGNED;
function "not" (L: SIGNED) return SIGNED;

-- Shift functions:
function SHIFT_LEFT (U : UNSIGNED; SIZE : NATURAL)
        return UNSIGNED;
function SHIFT_LEFT (S: SIGNED; SIZE : NATURAL)
        return SIGNED;
function SHIFT_RIGHT (U: UNSIGNED; SIZE : NATURAL)
        return UNSIGNED;
function SHIFT_RIGHT (S: SIGNED; SIZE : NATURAL)
        return SIGNED;

-- Preset / clear procedure:
procedure PRESET_CLEAR (signal FF: out UNSIGNED;
        PC_VALUE: UNSIGNED);
procedure PRESET_CLEAR (signal FF: out SIGNED;
        PC_VALUE: SIGNED);
procedure PRESET_CLEAR (signal FF: out INTEGER;
        PC_VALUE: INTEGER);
```

```
-- Clock-level functions:
function HIGH_LEVEL (CLK: STD_ULOGIC) return BOOLEAN;
function LOW_LEVEL (CLK: STD_ULOGIC) return BOOLEAN;

-- Utility function used in test benches:
function NOT_EQUALS (OBSERVED, EXPECTED : STD_ULOGIC)
          return BOOLEAN;

end package STD_LOGIC_ARITH;
```

❑

Appendix C

A Generic Library

This appendix describes a package GENERIC_COMP that contains a list of generic component declarations. These components are used in the synthesized netlists shown or described in this text. Functionality of each component is described using comments.

```
-- This package resides in library SYNTH.
--
library IEEE;
use IEEE.STD_LOGIC_1164.all;
package GENERIC_COMP is

    component AND2
        -- Z <= A and B;
        port (A, B: in STD_ULOGIC;
             Z: out STD_ULOGIC);
    end component;
```

```
component AOI21
    -- Z <= not ((A1 and A2) or B);
  port (A1, A2, B: in STD_ULOGIC;
      Z: out STD_ULOGIC);
end component;

component AOI211
    -- Z <= not ((A1 and A2) or B1 or B2);
  port (A1, A2, B1, B2: in STD_ULOGIC;
      Z: out STD_ULOGIC);
end component;

component AOI22
    -- Z <= not ((A1 and A2) or (B1 and B2));
  port (A1, A2, B1, B2: in STD_ULOGIC;
      Z: out STD_ULOGIC);
end component;

component BN20T20D
    -- Bidirectional buffer.
    -- Z <= PADI;
    -- PADO <= '0' when A='0' and STN='0' else
    --          '1' when A='1' and ST='1' else
    --          'Z';
  port (A, ST, STN, PADI: in STD_ULOGIC;
      Z, PADO: out STD_ULOGIC);
end component;

component BUF
    -- Z <= A;
  port (A: in STD_ULOGIC;
      Z: out STD_ULOGIC);
end component;

component FD1P3AX
    -- Positive edge-triggered, positive-level sample,
    -- static D-type FF.
  port (D, SP, CK: in STD_ULOGIC;
      Q, QN: out STD_ULOGIC);
end component;

component FD1S1A
    -- Positive-level sense static D-type FF (latch).
  port (D, CK: in STD_ULOGIC;
      Q, QN: out STD_ULOGIC);
end component;
```

component FD1S1B
    -- Positive-level sense, positive asynchronous preset,
    -- static D-type FF (latch).
  port (D, CK, PD: **in** STD_ULOGIC;
      Q, QN: **out** STD_ULOGIC);
end component;

component FD1S1D
    -- Positive-level sense, positive asynchronous clear,
    -- static D-type FF (latch).
  port (D, CK, CD: **in** STD_ULOGIC;
      Q, QN: **out** STD_ULOGIC);
end component;

component FD1S1F
    -- Positive-level sense, negative asynchronous clear,
    -- positive asynchronous preset, static D-type FF (latch).
  port (D, CK, PD, CDN: **in** STD_ULOGIC;
      Q, QN: **out** STD_ULOGIC);
end component;

component FD1S2AX
    -- Negative edge-triggered, static D-type FF.
  port (D, CK: **in** STD_ULOGIC;
      Q, QN: **out** STD_ULOGIC);
end component;

component FD1S2BX
    -- Negative edge-triggered, positive asynchronous preset,
    -- static D-type FF.
  port (D, CK, PD: **in** STD_ULOGIC;
      Q, QN: **out** STD_ULOGIC);
end component;

component FD1S2CX
    -- Negative edge-triggered, positive asynchronous preset,
    -- positive asynchronous clear, static D-type FF.
  port (D, CK, PD: **in** STD_ULOGIC;
      Q, QN: **out** STD_ULOGIC);
end component;

component FD1S2DX
    -- Negative edge-triggered, positive asynchronous clear,
    -- static D-type FF.
  port (D, CK, CD: **in** STD_ULOGIC;
      Q, QN: **out** STD_ULOGIC);

end component;

component FD1S2EX
    -- Negative edge-triggered, negative asynchronous clear,
    -- static D-type FF.
  port (D, CK, CDN: **in** STD_ULOGIC;
        Q, QN: **out** STD_ULOGIC);
end component;

component FD1S2FX
    -- Negative edge-triggered, negative asynchronous clear,
    -- positive asynchronous preset, static D-type FF.
  port (D, CK, PD, CDN: **in** STD_ULOGIC;
        Q, QN: **out** STD_ULOGIC);
end component;

component FD1S2GX
    -- Negative edge-triggered, negative asynchronous preset,
    -- static D-type FF.
  port (D, CK, PD, CDN: **in** STD_ULOGIC;
        Q, QN: **out** STD_ULOGIC);
end component;

component FD1S2IX
    -- Negative edge-triggered, positive synchronous clear,
    -- static D-type FF.
  port (D, CK, CD: **in** STD_ULOGIC;
        Q, QN: **out** STD_ULOGIC);
end component;

component FD1S2JX
    -- Negative edge-triggered, positive synchronous preset,
    -- static D-type FF.
  port (D, CK, PD: **in** STD_ULOGIC;
        Q, QN: **out** STD_ULOGIC);
end component;

component FD1S2NX
    -- Negative edge-triggered, positive asynchronous clear,
    -- negative asynchronous preset, static D-type FF.
  port (D, CK, PDN, CD: **in** STD_ULOGIC;
        Q, QN: **out** STD_ULOGIC);
end component;

component FD1S2OX
    -- Negative edge-triggered, positive synchronous clear,
    -- positive synchronous preset, static D-type FF.

```
    port (D, CK, PD, CD: in STD_ULOGIC;
        Q, QN: out STD_ULOGIC);
end component;

component FD1S3AX
    -- Positive edge-triggered, static D-type FF.
  port (D, CK: in STD_ULOGIC;
        Q, QN: out STD_ULOGIC);
end component;

component FD1S3BX
    -- Positive edge-triggered, positive asynchronous preset,
    -- static D-type FF.
  port (D, CK: in STD_ULOGIC;
        Q, QN: out STD_ULOGIC);
end component;

component FD1S3CX
    -- Positive edge-triggered, positive asynchronous clear,
    -- positive asynchronous preset, static D-type FF.
  port (D, CK: in STD_ULOGIC;
        Q, QN: out STD_ULOGIC);
end component;

component FD1S3EX
    -- Positive edge-triggered, negative synchronous clear,
    -- static D-type FF.
  port (D, CK, CDN: in STD_ULOGIC;
        Q, QN: out STD_ULOGIC);
end component;

component FL1S2AX
    -- Negative edge-triggered, data select front end, scan FF.
  port (D0, D1, CK, SD: in STD_ULOGIC;
        Q, QN: out STD_ULOGIC);
end component;

component FL1S2EX
    -- Negative edge-triggered, data select front end,
    -- negative asynchronous clear, scan FF.
  port (D0, D1, CK, SD, CDN: in STD_ULOGIC;
        Q, QN: out STD_ULOGIC);
end component;

component FL1S3AX
    -- Positive edge-triggered, data select front end, scan FF.
  port (D0, D1, CK, SD: in STD_ULOGIC;
```

```
            Q, QN: out STD_ULOGIC);
end component;

component FL1S3CX
      -- Positive edge-triggered, data select front end, positive asynchronous
      -- clear, positive asynchronous preset, scan FF.
    port (D0, D1, CK, SD: in STD_ULOGIC;
            Q, QN: out STD_ULOGIC);
end component;

component FL1S3EX
      -- Positive edge-triggered, data select front end,
      -- negative asynchronous clear, scan FF.
    port (D0, D1, CK, SD, CDN: in STD_ULOGIC;
            Q, QN: out STD_ULOGIC);
end component;

component FS0S1D
      -- Positive-level S input, positive-level R input,
      -- positive asynchronous clear, R-S FF (latch).
    port (S, R, CD: in STD_ULOGIC;
            Q, QN: out STD_ULOGIC);
end component;

component INRB
      -- Z <= not A;
    port (A: in STD_ULOGIC;
          Z: out STD_ULOGIC);
end component;

component ND2
      -- Z <= A nand B;
    port (A, B: in STD_ULOGIC;
          Z: out STD_ULOGIC);
end component;

component ND3
      -- Z <= not (A and B and C);
    port (A, B, C: in STD_ULOGIC;
          Z: out STD_ULOGIC);
end component;

component ND4
      -- Z <= not (A and B and C and D);
    port (A, B, C, D: in STD_ULOGIC;
          Z: out STD_ULOGIC);
end component;
```

```vhdl
component NR2
    -- Z <= not (A or B);
  port (A, B: in STD_ULOGIC;
      Z: out STD_ULOGIC);
end component;

component NR3
    -- Z <= not (A or B or C);
  port (A, B, C: in STD_ULOGIC;
      Z: out STD_ULOGIC);
end component;

component NR4
    -- Z <= not (A or B or C or D);
  port (A, B, C, D: in STD_ULOGIC;
      Z: out STD_ULOGIC);
end component;

component OAI21
    -- Z <= not ((A1 or A2) and B);
  port (A1, A2, B: in STD_ULOGIC;
      Z: out STD_ULOGIC);
end component;

component OAI22
    -- Z <= not ((A1 or A2) and (B1 or B2));
  port (A1, A2, B1, B2: in STD_ULOGIC;
      Z: out STD_ULOGIC);
end component;

component OAI4321
    -- Z <= not ((A1 or A2 or A3 or A4) and (B1 or B2 or B3)
    --     and (C1 and C2) and D);
  port (A1, A2, A3, A4, B1, B2, B3, C1, C2, D: in STD_ULOGIC;
      Z: out STD_ULOGIC);
end component;

component OR2
    -- Z <= A or B;
  port (A, B: in STD_ULOGIC;
      Z: out STD_ULOGIC);
end component;

component OR4
    -- Z <= A or B or C or D;
  port (A, B, C, D: in STD_ULOGIC;
```

```
        Z: out STD_ULOGIC);
end component;

component TBUS
    -- Q <= 'Z' when CK = '0' and CKN = '1',
    --       '0' when CK = '1' and D = '0',
    --       '1' when CKN = '0' and D = '1';
   port (D, CK, CKN: in STD_ULOGIC;
        Q: out STD_ULOGIC);
end component;

component XNOR2
    -- Z <= not (A xor B);
   port (A, B: in STD_ULOGIC;
        Z: out STD_ULOGIC);
end component;

component XOR2
    -- Z <= A xor B;
   port (A, B: in STD_ULOGIC;
        Z: out STD_ULOGIC);
end component;

component XOR2Z
    -- Z <= A xor B; Z1 <= not (A or B);
   port (A, B: in STD_ULOGIC;
        Z, Z1: out STD_ULOGIC);
end component;

end GENERIC_COMP;
```

□

Bibliography

Here is a select list of suggested readings and books on the VHDL language and on VHDL synthesis.

1. Airiau R., et. al., *Circuit Synthesis with VHDL*, Boston: Kluwer Academic, 1994.

2. Armstrong, J. R., *Chip-level Modeling with VHDL*, Englewood Cliffs, NJ: Prentice Hall, 1988.

3. Ashenden, P.J., *The Designers Guide to VHDL*, Morgan Kaufmann, 1995.

4. Ashenden, P.J., *The VHDL Cookbook*, The University of Adelaide, Australia, 1990.

5. Baker, L., *VHDL Programming with Advanced Topics*, John Wiley and Sons, Inc., 1993.

6. Berge, J-M., et al., *VHDL Designer's Reference*, Kluwer Academic, 1992.

7. Berge, J-M., et al., *VHDL'92*, Kluwer Academic, 1993.

232   Bibliography

8.   Bhasker, J., *A VHDL Primer*, Englewood Cliffs, NJ: Prentice Hall, 1992.

9.   Bhasker, J., *A VHDL Primer: Revised edition*, Englewood Cliffs, NJ: Prentice Hall, 1995.

10.   Bhasker, J., *A Guide to VHDL Syntax*, Englewood Cliffs, NJ: Prentice Hall, 1995.

11.   Bhasker, J., *VHDL: Features and Applications*, A self-study course, IEEE, 1995.

12.   Bhasker, J., *Process-Graph Analyzer: A Front-end Tool for VHDL Behavioral Synthesis*, Software Practice and Experience, vol. 18, no. 5, May 1988.

13.   Bhasker, J., *An Algorithm for Microcode Compaction of VHDL Behavioral Descriptions*, Proc. 20th Microprogramming Workshop, December 1987.

14.   Coelho, D., *The VHDL Handbook*, Boston: Kluwer Academic, 1988.

15.   Cohen, Ben, *VHDL Coding Styles and Methodologies*, Boston: Kluwer Academic, 1995.

16.   De Micheli, G., R.K. Brayton and A. Sangiovanni Vincentelli, *Optimal State Assignment for Finite State Machines*, IEEE Transactions on CAD, CAD-4(3), pp269-284, July 1985.

17.   Harr, R., and A. Stanculescu (eds.), *Applications of VHDL to Circuit Design*, Boston: Kluwer Academic, 1991.

18.   Hsu, Y-C., et. al., *VHDL Modeling for Digital Design Synthesis*, Boston: Kluwer Academic, 1995.

19.   *IEEE Standard VHDL Language Reference Manual, Std 1076-1993*, IEEE, NY, 1993.

20.   *IEEE Standard Multivalue Logic System for VHDL Model Interoperability (Std_Logic_1164)*, Std 1164-1993, IEEE, 1993.

21.   Kurup, Pran and T. Abbasi, *Logic Synthesis Using Synopsys*, Boston: Kluwer Academic, 1995.

22.   Lipsett, R., et. al., *VHDL: Hardware Description and Design*, Boston: Kluwer Academic, 1989.

23.   Navabi, Z., *VHDL Analysis and Modeling of Digital Systems*, McGraw Hill, 1993.

24.   Ott, D.E. and T.J. Wilderotter, *A Designer's Guide to VHDL Synthesis*, Boston: Kluwer Academic, 1994.

25. Perry, D., *VHDL*, New York: McGraw Hill, 1991.

26. Schoen, J.M., *Performance and Fault Modeling with VHDL*, Englewood Cliffs, NJ: Prentice Hall, 1992.

❏

Index

❏